The Tanner Lectures on Human Values

THE TANNER LECTURES ON HUMAN VALUES

VI

1985

Nadine Gordimer, Leonard B. Meyer, Stephen Jay Gould,
Donald D. Brown, Georg Henrik von Wright,
Helmut Schmidt

Sterling M. McMurrin, *Editor*

University of Utah Press — Salt Lake City
Cambridge University Press — Cambridge, London, Melbourne, Sydney

Published in North and South America
and the Philippines
by the University of Utah Press,
Salt Lake City, Utah 84112, U.S.A.,
and in Great Britain and all other countries by
The Press Syndicate of the University of Cambridge
The Edinburgh Building, Shaftesbury Road,
Cambridge CB2 2RU, and
296 Beaconsfield Parade, Middle Park, Melbourne 3206
Australia.

The paper in this book meets the standards
for permanence and durability established by
the Committee on Production Guidelines for Book Longevity
of the Council on Library Resources.

THE TANNER LECTURES ON HUMAN VALUES

Appointment as a Tanner lecturer is a recognition of uncommon capabilities and outstanding scholarly or leadership achievement in the field of human values. The lecturers may be drawn from philosophy, religion, the humanities and sciences, the creative arts and learned professions, or from leadership in public or private affairs. The lectureships are international and intercultural and transcend ethnic, national, religious, or ideological distinctions.

The purpose of the Tanner Lectures is to advance and reflect upon the scholarly and scientific learning relating to human values and valuation. This purpose embraces the entire range of values pertinent to the human condition, interest, behavior, and aspiration.

The Tanner Lectures were formally founded on July 1, 1978, at Clare Hall, Cambridge University. They were established by the American scholar, industrialist, and philanthropist, Obert Clark Tanner. In creating the lectureships, Professor Tanner said, "I hope these lectures will contribute to the intellectual and moral life of mankind. I see them simply as a search for a better understanding of human behavior and human values. This understanding may be pursued for its own intrinsic worth, but it may also eventually have practical consequences for the quality of personal and social life."

Permanent Tanner lectureships, with lectures given annually, are established at six institutions: Clare Hall, Cambridge University; Harvard University; Brasenose College, Oxford University; Stanford University; the University of Michigan; and the University of Utah. Each year lectureships may be granted to not more than four additional colleges or universities for one year only. The institutions are selected by the Trustees in consultation with an Advisory Commission.

The sponsoring institutions have full autonomy in the appointment of their lecturers. A major purpose of the lecture program is the publication and wide distribution of the Lectures in an annual volume.

The Tanner Lectures on Human Values is a nonprofit corporation administered at the University of Utah under the direction of a self-perpetuating, international Board of Trustees and with the advice and counsel of an Advisory Commission. The Trustees meet annually to enact policies that will ensure the quality of the lectureships.

The entire lecture program, including the costs of administration, is fully and generously funded in perpetuity by an endowment of the University of Utah by Professor Tanner and Mrs. Grace Adams Tanner.

Obert C. Tanner was born in Farmington, Utah, in 1904. He was educated at the University of Utah, Harvard University, and Stanford University. He has served on the faculty of Stanford University and is presently Emeritus Professor of Philosophy at the University of Utah. He is the founder and chairman of the O. C. Tanner Company, manufacturing jewelers.

STERLING M. McMURRIN
University of Utah

THE ADVISORY COMMISSION

DEREK C. BOK
President of Harvard University

HAROLD T. SHAPIRO
President of the University of Michigan

DONALD KENNEDY
President of Stanford University

CONTENTS

The Tanner Lectures on Human Values v

The Trustees vii

The Advisory Commission viii

Preface to Volume VI xi

Nadine Gordimer   The Essential Gesture: Writers
          and Responsibility 1

Leonard B. Meyer   Music and Ideology in the
          Nineteenth Century 21

Stephen Jay Gould   Challenges to Neo-Darwinism and Their
          Meaning for a Revised View
          of Human Consciousness 53

Donald D. Brown   The Impact of Modern Genetics....... 75

          I. Genetic Engineering: Its Promise
          and Problems 77

          II. How New Methods in Biology
          Are Solving Old Problems 94

Georg Henrik
* von Wright*   Of Human Freedom 107

Helmut Schmidt   The Future of the Atlantic Alliance 171

The Tanner Lecturers 197

Index 201

PREFACE

The Tanner Lectures on Human Values were formally established in 1978 by a Board of Trustees convened at Clare Hall, Cambridge University. Since then annual lectures have been delivered at the six institutions where permanent lectureships were established: Clare Hall, Cambridge University; Harvard University; Brasenose College, Oxford University; Stanford University; the University of Michigan; and the University of Utah. In addition, lectures have been delivered at Utah State University, the Hebrew University of Jerusalem, Australian National University, Jawaharlal Nehru University, and the University of Helsinki. It is the policy of the Tanner Trustees to publish these lectures in an annual volume. Accordingly, the present volume includes the lectures read by Professor Georg Henrik von Wright at the University of Helsinki in addition to those delivered during the academic year 1983–84 at the institutions which receive permanent funding. A general index to volumes I through V is included in Volume V.

A lectureship has been established for 1984–85 at the Queens University of Belfast, Ireland. This lecture, together with those which are delivered during the academic year 1984–85, will be published in Volume VII of the Tanner Lectures. (Nadine Gordimer's lecture, delivered early in the academic year, is published in this volume.)

It is the intention of the Trustees to continue funding and publishing special lectureships at selected universities in the years ahead in addition to the papers read under the permanent lectureships.

There are several lectureships administered by the Trustees of the Tanner Lectures on Human Values and funded by the Tanner endowment which are not included in the annual volumes of Tanner Lectures. These are published independently by the institutions where the lectureships are established.

The Essential Gesture:
Writers and Responsibility

NADINE GORDIMER

THE TANNER LECTURES ON HUMAN VALUES

Delivered at
The University of Michigan

October 12, 1984

NADINE GORDIMER was born and lives in South Africa. She is the author of eight novels, including *July's People*, *Burger's Daughter*, and *The Conservationist* — which won England's Booker Prize in 1974 — as well as eight collections of short stories, the most recent of which is *Something Out There*, published in 1984. Among Ms. Gordimer's other literary awards is the French international prize the Grand Aigle d'Or (1975), and she was awarded the Scottish Arts Council's Neil Gunn Fellowship for 1981.

When I began to write, at the age of nine or ten, I did so in what I have come to believe is the only real innocence — an act without responsibility. For one has only to watch very small children playing together to see how the urge to influence, exact submission, defend dominance, gives away the presence of natal human 'sin' whose punishment is the burden of responsibility. I was alone. My poem or story came out of myself I did not know how. It was directed at no one, was read by no one.

Responsibility is what awaits outside the Eden of creativity. I should never have dreamt that this most solitary and deeply marvellous of secrets — the urge *to make* with words — would become a vocation for which the world, and that lifetime lodger, conscionable self-awareness, would claim the right to call me and all my kind to account. The creative act is not pure. History evidences it. Ideology demands it. Society exacts it. The writer loses Eden, writes to be read, and comes to realize that he is answerable. The writer is *held responsible*: and the verbal phrase is ominously accurate, for the writer not only has laid upon him responsibility for various interpretations of the consequences of his work, he is 'held' before he begins by the claims of different concepts of morality — artistic, linguistic, ideological, national, political, religious — asserted upon him. He learns that his creative act was not pure even while being formed in his brain: already it carried congenital responsibility for what preceded cognition and volition: for what he represented in genetic, environmental, social, and economic terms when he was born of his parents.

Roland Barthes wrote that language is a 'corpus of prescriptions and habits common to all the writers of a period.' [1]

---

[1] Roland Barthes, *Writing Degree Zero*.

[3]

He also wrote that a writer's 'enterprise' — his work — is his 'essential gesture as a social being.'

Between these two statements I have found my subject, which is their tension and connection: the writer's responsibility. For language — language as the transformation of thought into written words in any language — is not only 'a' but *the* corpus common to all writers in our period. (Perhaps to a lesser extent this has been so in others, but for reasons arising out of those periods and not ours.) From the corpus of language, within that guild shared with fellow writers, the writer fashions his enterprise, which then becomes his 'essential gesture as a social being.' Created in the common lot of language, that essential gesture is individual; and with it the writer quits the commune of the corpus; but with it he enters the commonalty of society, the world of other beings who are not writers. He and his fellow writers are at once isolated from one another far and wide by the varying concepts, in different societies, of what the essential gesture of the writer as a social being is.

By comparison of what is expected of them, writers often have little or nothing in common. There is no responsibility arising out of the status of the writer as a social being that could call upon Saul Bellow, Kurt Vonnegut, Susan Sontag, Toni Morrison, or John Berger to write on a subject that would result in their being silenced under a ban, banished to internal exile, or detained in jail. But in the Soviet Union, South Africa, Iran, Vietnam, Taiwan, certain Latin American and other countries, this is the kind of demand that responsibility for the social significance of being a writer exacts: a double demand, the first from the oppressed, to act as spokesperson for them, the second, from the state, to take punishment for that act. Conversely, it is not conceivable that a Molly Keane, or any other writer of the quaint Gothic-domestic cult presently discovered by discerning critics and readers in the United States as well as Britain, would be taken seriously in terms of the interpretations of the 'essential gesture as a social being' called forth in countries such as the Soviet Union, South Africa, etc., if he or she lived there.

Yet those critics and readers who live safe from the realm of midnight arrests and solitary confinement that is the dark condominium of East and West have their demands upon the writer from such places, too. For them, his essential gesture as a social being is to take risks they themselves do not know if they would.

This results in strange and unpleasant distortions in the personality of some of these safe people. Any writer from a country of conflict will bear me out. When interviewed abroad, there is often disappointment that you are there, and not in jail in your own country. And since you are not — why are you not? Aha . . . does this mean you have not written the book you should have written? Can you imagine this kind of self-righteous inquisition being directed against a John Updike for not having made the trauma of America's Vietnam war the theme of his work?[2]

There is another tack of suspicion. The London *Daily Telegraph* reviewer of my recent book of stories said I must be exaggerating: if my country really was a place where such things happened, how was it I could write about them? And then there is the wish-fulfilment distortion, arising out of the homebody's projection of his dreams upon the exotic writer: the journalist who makes a bogus hero out of the writer who knows that the pen, where he lives, is a weapon not mightier than the sword.

One thing is clear: ours is a period when few can claim the absolute value of a writer without reference to a context of responsibilities. Exile as a mode of genius no longer exists; in place of Joyce we have the fragments of works appearing in *Index on*

[2] American society does not demand this 'orthodoxy' of its writers, because (arguably) its values are not in a crisis of survival concentrated on a single moral issue. Which does not authorize self-appointed cultural commissars to decide whether or not writers from other countries are fulfilling their 'essential gesture' in their own societies.

Censorship. These are the rags of suppressed literatures, translated from a Babel of languages; the broken cries of real exiles, not those who have rejected their homeland but who have been forced out — of their language, their culture, their society. In place of Joyce we have two of the best contemporary writers in the world, Czeslaw Milosz and Milan Kundera; but both regard themselves as amputated sensibilities, not free of Poland and Czechoslovakia in the sense that Joyce was free of Ireland — whole: out in the world but still in possession of the language and culture of home. In place of Joyce we have, one might argue, at least Borges; but in his old age, and out of what he sees in his blindness as he did not when he could see, for years now he has spoken wistfully of a desire to trace the trails made by ordinary lives instead of the arcane pattern of abstract forces of which they are the fingerpainting. Despite his rejection of ideologies (earning the world's inescapable and maybe accurate shove over to the ranks of the Right) even he senses on those lowered lids the responsibilities that feel out for writers so persistently in our time.

What right has society to impose responsibility upon writers and what right has the writer to resist? I want to examine not what is forbidden us by censorship — I know that story too well — but to what we are bidden. I want to consider what is expected of us by the dynamic of collective conscience and the will to liberty in various circumstances and places; whether we should respond, and if so, how we do.

'It is from the moment when I shall no longer be more than a writer that I shall cease to write.' [3] One of the great of our period, Camus, could say that. In theory, at least, as a writer he accepted the basis of the most extreme and pressing demand of our time. The ivory tower was finally stormed; and it was not with a white flag that the writer came out, but with manifesto unfurled and

---

[3] Albert Camus, *Carnets*.

arms crooked to link with the elbows of the people. And it was not just as their chronicler that the compact was made; the greater value, you will note, was placed on the persona outside of 'writer': to be 'no more than a writer' was to put an end to the justification for the very existence of the persona of 'writer'. Although the aphorism in its characteristically French neatness appears to wrap up all possible meanings of its statement, it does not. Camus' decision is a hidden as well as a revealed one. It is not just that he has weighed within himself his existential value as a writer against that of other functions as a man among men, and found independently in favour of the man; the scale has been set up by a demand outside himself, by his world situation. He has, in fact, accepted its condition that the greater responsibility is to society and not to art.

Long before it was projected into that of a world war, and again after the war, Camus' *natal* societal situation was that of a writer in the conflict of Western world decolonisation — the moral question of race and power by which the twentieth century will be characterized along with its discovery of the satanic ultimate in power, the means of human self-annihilation. But the demand made upon him and the moral imperative it set up in himself are those of a writer anywhere where the people he lives among, or any sections of them marked out by race or colour or religion, are discriminated against and repressed. Whether or not he himself materially belongs to the oppressed makes his assumption of extra-literary responsibility more or less 'natural', but does not alter much the problem of the conflict between integrities.

Loyalty is an emotion, integrity a conviction adhered to out of moral values. Therefore I speak here not of loyalties but integrities, in my recognition of society's right to make demands on the writer as equal to that of the writer's commitment to his artistic vision; the source of conflict is what demands are made and how they should be met.

The closest to reconciliation that I know of comes in my own country, South Africa, among some black writers. It certainly cannot be said to have occurred in the position of two of Africa's most important writers from elsewhere, Chinua Achebe and Wole Soyinka. They became 'more than writers' in answer to their country's — Nigeria's — crisis of civil war; but in no sense did the demand develop their creativity. On the contrary, both sacrificed for some years the energy of their creativity to the demands of activism, which included, for Soyinka, imprisonment. The same might be said of Ernesto Cardenal. But it is out of being 'more than a writer' that many black men and women in South Africa *begin* to write. All the obstacles and diffidences — lack of education, of a tradition of literary expression, even of the chance to form the everyday habit of reading that germinates a writer's gift — are overcome by the imperative to give expression to a majority not silent, but whose deeds and whose proud and angry volubility against suffering have not been given the eloquence of the written word. For these writers, there is no opposition of inner and outer demands. At the same time as they are writing, they are political activists in the concrete sense, teaching, proselytizing, organizing. When they are detained without trial it may be for what they have written, but when they are tried and convicted of crimes of conscience it is for what they have done as 'more than a writer'. 'Africa, my beginning . . . Africa my end' — these lines of the epic poem (banned in South Africa) written by Ngoapele Madingoane epitomise this synthesis of creativity and social responsibility;[4] what moves him, and the way it moves him, are perfectly at one with his society's demands. Without those demands he is not a poet.

The Marxist critic Ernst Fischer reaches anterior to my interpretation of this response with his proposition that 'the artist who

---

[4] Ngoapele Madingoane, *Africa My Beginning.*

belonged to a coherent society [here, read preconquest South Africa] and to a class that was not yet an impediment to progress [here, read not yet infected by white bourgeois aspirations] did not feel it any loss of artistic freedom if a certain range of subjects was prescribed to him' since such subjects were imposed 'usually by tendencies and traditions deeply rooted in the people'.[5] Of course, this may provide, in general, a sinister pretext for a government to invoke certain tendencies and traditions to suit its purpose of proscribing writers' themes, but applied to black writers in South Africa, history evidences the likely truth of the proposition. Their tendency and tradition for more than three hundred years has been to free themselves of white domination.

Art is on the side of the oppressed. Think before you shudder at the simplistic dictum and its heretical definition of the freedom of art. For if art is freedom of the spirit, how can it exist within the oppressors? And there is some evidence that it ceases to. What writer of any literary worth defends fascism, totalitarianism, racism, in an age when these are still pandemic? Ezra Pound is dead. In Poland, where are the poets who sing the epic of the men who have broken Solidarity? In South Africa, where are the writers who produce brilliant defences of apartheid?

It remains difficult to dissect the tissue between those for whom writing is a revolutionary activity no different from and to be practised concurrently with running a political trade union or making a false passport for someone on the run, and those who interpret their society's demand to be 'more than a writer' as something that may yet be fulfilled through the nature of their writing itself. Whether this latter interpretation is possible depends on the society within which the writer functions. Even 'only' to write may be to be 'more than a writer' for one such as Milan Kundera, who goes on writing what he sees and knows from within his situa-

[5] Ernst Fischer, *The Necessity of Art.*

tion — his country under repression — until a ban on publishing his books strips him of his 'essential gesture' of being a writer at all. Like one of his own characters, he must clean windows or sell tickets in a cinema booth for a living. That, ironically, is what being 'more than a writer' would come down to for him, if he were to have opted to stay on in his country — something I don't think Camus quite visualized. There are South Africans who have found themselves in the same position — for example, the poet Don Mattera, who for seven years was banned from writing, publishing, and even from reading his work in public. But in a country of total repression of the majority, like South Africa, where literature is nevertheless only half-suppressed because the greater part of that black majority is kept semi-literate and cannot be affected by books, there is — just — the possibility for a writer to be 'only' a writer, in terms of activity, and yet 'more than a writer' in terms of fulfilling the demands of his society. An honourable category has been found for him. As 'cultural worker' in the race/class struggle he still may be seen to serve, even if he won't march towards the teargas and bullets.

In this context, long before the term 'cultural worker' was taken over from the vocabulary of other revolutions, black writers had to accept the social responsibility white ones didn't have to — that of being the only historians of events among their people; Dhlomo, Plaatje, Mofolo, created characters who brought to life and preserved events either unrecorded by white historians or recorded purely from the point of view of white conquest.[6] From this beginning there has been a logical intensification of the demands of social responsibility, as over decades discrimination and repression set into law and institution, and resistance became a liberation struggle. This process culminated during the black uprising of 1976, calling forth poetry and prose in an impetus of

---

[6] H. I. E. Dhlomo, *Valley of a Thousand Hills*, and others; Solomon T. Plaatje, *Mhudi, Native Life in South Africa, Boer War Diary*; Thomas Mofolo, *Chaka*.

events not yet exhausted nor fully explored by writers. The uprising began as a revolt of youth and it brought a new consciousness — bold, incantatory, messianically reckless — to writers. It
also placed new demands upon them in the essential gesture that
bound them to a people springing about on the balls of their feet
before dawn-streaks of freedom and the threat of death. Private
emotions were inevitably outlawed by political activists who had
no time for any; black writers were expected to prove their black-
ness *as a revolutionary condition* by submitting to an unwritten
orthodoxy of interpretation and representation in their work. I
stress unwritten because there was no Writers' Union to be ex-
pelled from. But there was a company of political leaders, intel-
lectuals, and the new category of the alert young, shaming others
with their physical and mental bravery, to ostracise a book of
poems or prose if it were to be found irrelevant to the formal
creation of an image of a people anonymously, often spontane-
ously heroic.

Some of my friends among black writers have insisted to me
that this 'imposition' of orthodoxy is a white interpretation; that
the impulse came from within to discard the lantern of artistic
truth that reveals human worth through human ambiguity, and to
see by the flames of burning vehicles only the strong, thick lines
that draw heroes. To gain his freedom the writer must give up
his freedom. Whether the impulse came from within, without, or
both, for the black South African writer it became an imperative
to attempt that salvation. It remains so; but in the 1980s many
black writers of quality have come into conflict with the demand
from without — responsibility as orthodoxy — and have begun to
negotiate the right to their own, inner interpretation of the essential gesture by which they are part of the black struggle.[7] The
black writer's revolutionary responsibility may be posited by him

[7] Among the most recent examples, Njabulo Ndebele's *Fools*, and Ahmed
Essop's *The Emperor*.

as the discovery, in his own words, of the revolutionary spirit for
the present in the rescue — for the post-revolutionary future —
of that nobility in ordinary men and women to be found only
among their doubts, culpabilities, shortcomings: their courage-in-
spite-of.

To whom are South African writers answerable in their essential gesture if they are not in the historical and existential situation
of blacks, and if (axiomatic for them in varying degrees) they are
alienated from their 'own', the historical and existential situation
of whites there? Only a section of blacks places any demands
upon white writers at all; that grouping within radical blacks
which grants integrity to whites who declare themselves for the
black freedom struggle. To be one of these writers is firstly to be
presented with a political responsibility if not an actual orthodoxy:
the white writer's task as cultural worker is to raise the consciousness of white people, who, unlike himself, have not woken up. It
is a responsibility at once minor, in comparison with that placed
upon the black writer as composer of battle hymns, and yet for-
bidding if one compares the honour and welcome that await the
black writer, from blacks, and the branding as traitor, or, at best,
turned backside of indifference that await the white, from the
white establishment. With fortunate irony, however, it is a responsibility which the white writer already has taken on, for himself, if the other responsibility — to his creative integrity — keeps
him scrupulous in writing about what he knows to be true whether
whites like to hear it or not: for the majority of his readers are
white. He brings some influence to bear on whites though not on
the white-dominated government; he may influence those individuals who are already coming-to bewilderedly out of the trip of
power, and those who gain courage from reading the open expression of their own suppressed rebellion. I doubt whether the white
writer, even if giving expression to the same themes as blacks, has
much social use in inspiriting blacks, or is needed to. Sharing the

life of the black ghettoes is the primary qualification the white writer lacks, so far as populist appreciation is concerned. But black writers do share with white the same kind of influence on those whites who read them; and so the categories that the state would keep apart get mixed through literature — an unforeseen 'essential gesture' of writers in their social responsibility in a divided country.

The white writer who has declared himself answerable to the oppressed people is not expected by them to be 'more than a writer', since his historical position is not seen as allowing him to be central to the black struggle. But a few writers have challenged this definition by taking upon themselves exactly the same revolutionary responsibilities as black writers such as Alex la Guma, Dennis Brutus, and Mongane Serote, who make no distinction between the tasks of underground activity and writing a story or poem. Like Brutus, the white writers Breyten Breytenbach and Jeremy Cronin were tried and imprisoned for accepting the necessity they saw for being 'more than a writer'. Their interpretation of a writer's responsibility, in their country and situation, remains a challenge, particularly to those who disagree with their action while sharing with them the politics of opposition to repression. There is no moral authority like that of sacrifice.

In South Africa the ivory tower is bulldozed anew with every black man's home destroyed to make way for a white man's. Yet there are positions between the bulldozed ivory tower and the maximum security prison. The one who sees his responsibility in being 'only a writer' has still to decide whether this means he can fulfil his essential gesture to society only by ready-packaging his creativity to the dimensions of a social realism *those who will free him of his situation* have the authority to ask of him, or whether he may be able to do so by work the Western liberal George Steiner defines as 'scrupulously argued, not declaimed . . . informed, at each node and articulation of proposal, with a just

sense of the complex, contradictory nature of historical evidence'.[8]
The great mentor of Russian revolutionary writers of the nineteenth century, Belinsky, advises, 'Do not worry about the incarna-
tion of ideas. If you are a poet, your works will contain them without your knowledge — they will be both moral and national if you
follow your inspiration freely'.[9] Octavio Paz, speaking from Mexico for the needs of the Third World, sees a fundamental function
as social critic for the writer who is 'only a writer'.[10] It is a responsibility that goes back to source: the corpus of language from
which the writer arises. 'Social criticism begins with grammar and
the re-establishment of meanings'. This was the responsibility
taken up in the post-Nazi era by Heinrich Böll and Günter Grass,
and is presently being fulfilled by South African writers, black and
white, in exposing the real meaning of the South African government's vocabulary of racist euphemisms — such terms as 'separate
development', 'resettlement', 'national states', and its grammar of
a racist legislature, with segregated chambers for whites, so-called
coloureds and Indians, and no representation whatever for the
majority of South Africans, those classified as black.

If the writer accepts the social realist demand, from without,
will he be distorting, paradoxically, the very ability he has to offer
the creation of a new society? If he accepts the other, self-imposed
responsibility, how far into the immediate needs of his society will
he reach? Will hungry people find revelation in the ideas his work
contains 'without his knowledge'? The one certainty, in South
Africa as a specific historical situation, is that there is no opting
out of the two choices. Outside is a culture in sterile decay, its

---

[8] George Steiner, reviewing E. M. Cioran's *Drawn and Quartered* in *The New Yorker*, April 16, 1984.

[9] Vissarion Belinsky, 1810–1848. The quote is from my notebooks, and I am unable to verify its original source.

[10] Octavio Paz, 'Development and Other Mirages', from *The Other Mexico: Critique of the Pyramid*.

achievements culminating in the lines of tin toilets set up in the veld for people 'resettled' by force. Whether a writer is black or white, in South Africa the essential gesture by which he enters the brotherhood of man — white is the only definition of society that has any permanent validity — is a revolutionary gesture.

'Has God ever expressed an opinion?' — Flaubert, writing to George Sand. 'I believe that great art is impersonal. . . . I want neither love nor hatred nor pity nor anger. The impartiality of description would then become equal to the majesty of the law'.

Nearly a century passed before the *nouveau roman* writers attempted this kind of majesty, taking over from another medium the mode of still-life. The work aspired to be the object-in-itself, although made up of elements — words, images — that can never be lifted from the 'partiality' of countless connotations. The writers went as far as it is possible to go from any societal demand. They had tried so hard that their vision became fixed on Virginia Woolf's mark on the wall — and as an end, not a beginning. Yet the anti-movement seems to have been, after all, a negative variation on a kind of social responsibility some writers have assumed at least since the beginning of the modern movement: to transform the world by style. This was and is something that could not serve as the writer's essential gesture in countries such as South Africa and Nicaragua; but it has had its possibilities and sometimes proves its validity where complacency, indifference, accidie, and not conflict, threaten the human spirit. To transform the world by style was the iconoclastic essential gesture tried out by the Symbolists and Dadaists; but whatever social transformation (in shaping a new consciousness) they might have served in breaking old forms was horribly superseded by different means: Europe, the Far, Middle, and Near East, Asia, Latin America, and Africa overturned by wars; millions of human beings wandering without the basic structure of a roof.

The Symbolists' and Dadaists' successors, in what Susan Sontag terms 'the cultural revolution that refuses to be political' have among them their '. . . spiritual adventurers, social pariahs determined to disestablish themselves . . . not to be morally useful to the community' — the essential gesture withheld by Céline and Kerouac.[11] Responsibility reaches out into the manifesto, however, and claims the 'seers' of this revolution. Through a transformation by style — depersonalized laconicism of the word almost to the Word — Samuel Beckett takes on as his essential gesture a responsibility direct to human destiny, and not to any local cell of humanity. This is the assumption of a messenger of the gods rather than a cultural worker. It is a disestablishment from the temporal; yet some kind of final statement exacted by the temporal. Is Beckett the freest writer in the world, or is he the most responsible of all?

Kafka was also a seer, one who sought to transform consciousness by style, and who was making his essential gesture to human destiny rather than the European fragment of it to which he belonged. But he was unconscious of his desperate signal. He believed that the act of writing was one of detachment that moved writers 'with everything we possess, to the moon'.[12] He was unaware of the terrifyingly impersonal, apocalyptic, prophetic nature of his vision in that ante-room to his parents' bedroom in Prague. Beckett, on the contrary, has been signalled to and consciously responded. The summons came from his time. His place — not Warsaw, San Salvador, Soweto — has nothing specific to ask of him. And unlike Joyce, he can never be in exile wherever he chooses to live, because he has chosen to be answerable to the twentieth-century human condition which has its camp everywhere,

---

[11] Susan Sontag, 'Approaching Artaud', from *Under the Sign of Saturn*: '. . . authors . . . recognised by their effort to disestablish themselves, by their will not to be morally useful to the community, by their inclination to present themselves not as social critics but as seers, spiritual adventurers and social pariahs'.

[12] Franz Kafka, from a letter to Max Brod, quoted by Ronald Hayman in *Kafka*.

or nowhere — whichever way you see Vladimir, Estragon, Pozzo, and Lucky.

Writers who accept a professional responsibility in the transformation of society are always seeking ways of doing so that their societies could not ever imagine, let alone demand: asking of themselves means that will plunge like a drill to release the great primal spout of creativity, drench the censors, cleanse the statute books of their pornography of racist and sexist laws, hose down religious differences, extinguish napalm bombs and flame-throwers, wash away pollution from land, sea, and air, and bring out human beings into the occasional summer fount of naked joy. Each has his own dowsing twig, held over heart and brain. Michel Tournier sees writers' responsibilities as to 'disrupt the establishment in exact proportion to their creativity'.[13] This is a bold global responsibility, though more Orphic and terrestrial than Beckett's; more human, if you like. It also could be taken as admittance that this is *all* writers can do; for creativity comes from within, it cannot be produced by will or dictate if it is not there, although it can be crushed by dictate. Tournier's — this apparently fantastical and uncommitted writer's — own creativity is nevertheless so close to the people that he respects as a marvel — and makes it so for his readers — the daily history of their lives as revealed in city trash dumps. And he is so fundamentally engaged by what alienates human beings that he imagines for everyone the restoration of wholeness (the totality which revolutionary art seeks to create for alienated man) in a form of Being that both sexes experience as one — something closer to a classless society than to a sexually hermaphroditic curiosity.

The *transformation of experience* remains the writer's basic essential gesture; the lifting out of a limited category something that reveals its full meaning and significance only when the writ-

[13] Michel Tournier, *Gemini*.

er's imagination has expanded it. This has never been more evident than in the context of extreme experiences of sustained personal horror that are central to the period of twentieth-century writers. The English critic John Bayley writes of Anna Akhmatova:

> A violently laconic couplet at the end of the sections of *Requiem* records her husband dead, her son in prison. . . . It is as good an instance as any of the power of great poetry to generalize and speak for the human predicament in extremity, for in fact she had probably never loved Gumilev, from whom she had lived apart for years, and her son had been brought up by his grandmother. But the sentiment [of the poem] was not for herself but for 'her people', with whom she was at that time so totally united in suffering.[14]

Writers in South Africa who are 'only writers' are sometimes reproached by those, black and white, who are in practical revolutionary terms 'more than writers', for writing of events as if they themselves had been at the heart of action, endurance, and suffering. So far as black writers are concerned, even though the humiliations and deprivations of daily life under apartheid enjoin them, many of them were no more among the children under fire from the police in the seventies, or are living as Freedom Fighters in the bush, than Akhmatova was a heart-broken wife or a mother separated from a son she had nurtured. Given these circumstances, their claim to generalize and speak for a human predicament in extremity comes from the lesser or greater extent of their *ability to do so*; and the development of that ability is their responsibility towards those with whom they are united by this extrapolation of suffering and resistance. White writers who are 'only writers' are open to related reproach for 'stealing the lives of blacks' as good material. Their claim to this 'material' is the same as the black writers' at an important existential remove nobody would discount. Their essential gesture can be fulfilled only in the integ-

---

[14] John Bayley, London *Observer*, Oct. 31, 1976.

rity Chekhov demanded: 'to describe a situation so truthfully that the reader can no longer evade it'.[15]

The writer is eternally in search of entelechy in his relation to his society. Everywhere in the world, he needs to be left alone and at the same time to have a vital connection with others; needs artistic freedom and knows it cannot exist without its wider context; feels the two presences within — creative self-absorption and conscionable awareness — and must resolve whether these are locked in death-struggle, or are really foetuses in a twinship of fecundity. Will the world let him, and will he know how to be the ideal of the writer as a social being, Walter Benjamin's storyteller, the one 'who could let the wick of his life be consumed completely by the gentle flame of his story'? [16]

[15] Anton Chekhov, quoted by Isaiah Berlin in *Russian Thinkers*.

[16] Walter Benjamin, *Illuminations*.

Music and Ideology in the Nineteenth Century

LEONARD B. MEYER

THE TANNER LECTURES ON HUMAN VALUES

Delivered at
Stanford University

May 17 and 21, 1984

LEONARD B. MEYER (b. 1918) majored in philosophy as an undergraduate, first at Bard College and then at Columbia University. After World War II, he returned to Columbia, taking a master's degree in composition. His Ph.D. was earned at the University of Chicago in the Committee on the History of Culture. He studied composition with Karl Weigl, Otto Luening, Aaron Copland, and Stefan Wolpe. From 1946 to 1975, Professor Meyer taught at the University of Chicago, and in the fall of 1975 he accepted a position at the University of Pennsylvania, where he is Benjamin Franklin Professor of Music and the Humanities.

Mr. Meyer has published four books: *Emotion and Meaning in Music*; *The Rhythmic Structure of Music* (with Grosvenor Cooper); *Music, the Arts and Ideas*, which received the Gordon Laing Prize of the University of Chicago Press; and *Explaining Music: Essays and Explorations*. He has written articles dealing with the aesthetics and psychology of music, and with problems in the theory and history of music. His Tanner Lectures were taken from a work in progress — a book concerned with the nature of style and style change in music.

I

It seems probable that Western culture has from its beginnings been characterized by a tension between the claims of Apollonian classicism and those of Dionysian romanticism. Classicism has been distinguished by a valuing of shared conventions and established constraints, the coherence of closed forms and the clarity of explicit meanings. Romanticism, on the other hand, has been defined by a valuing of individual innovation and the yearning arising from potentiality, by the informality of open structures and the suggestiveness of implicit significance. And countless critics and historians of the arts have remarked upon these traits and upon the continuing oscillation from one of these general outlooks to the other.

Each romantic phase, like each classic one is, of course, different from all the others. Each romanticism has its specific stylistic constraints; each has a different history. But the Romanticism that we will be concerned with — the movement begun in the last part of the eighteenth century and continued into our own time — was not merely different in its constraints and its immediate past. Rather it constituted a radical departure. It differed from all the preceding romanticisms in this: instead of being but a phase within a periodic swing in the beliefs and attitudes of the artistic/intellectual community, this Romanticism formed part of a profound revolution in political, social, and ideological outlook. At its core was an unequivocal and uncompromising repudiation and rejection of a hierarchic social order based upon arbitrary, inherited class distinctions.

Although its roots extended back to the Renaissance and Reformation — for instance, to the growing emphasis upon the worth of the individual, the widening perspective fostered by the discovery of new lands and cultures, and the remarkable achievements of the natural sciences — the prime driving force of the latest Romanticism was political and social. As Rousseau, its most polemical and influential spokesman, explicitly avowed: "I had attained the insight that everything is at bottom dependent on political arrangements, that no matter what position one takes, a people will never be otherwise than what its form of government makes it." [1]

Rousseau's views are familiar — indeed, they have become part of cultural scuttlebutt. But they so profoundly affected the choices made by Romantic composers that a capsule summary is warranted. The one I give is by Allan Bloom, a political scientist:

> Man was born free, equal, selfsufficient, unprejudiced, and whole; now, at the end of history, he is in chains (ruled by other men or by laws he did not make), defined by relations of inequality (rich or poor, noble or commoner, master or slave), dependent, full of false opinions or superstitions, and divided between his inclinations and his duties. [2]

The repudiation of the *ancien régime* was by no means confined to social, political, and economic realms. Whatever was deemed arbitrary or artificial, grounded in convention or the basis for distinction and privilege was called into question.

In no realm of culture, however, was the repudiation of the artificial and the conventional more vehement and thoroughgoing than in the arts — as a brief sampling amply indicates.

> Anton Thibaut: ". . . how easy it is for art to become unnatural . . . and how often do we find music, laboriously composed by mere artifice, uninspired by any real spontaneous emotion . . . ." [3]

[1] *Confessions,* quoted in Ernst Cassirer, *Rousseau, Kant, Goethe* (Princeton, 1945), p. 27.

[2] "The Education of Democratic Man: *Emile,*" *Rousseau in Our Time,* S. R. Graubard, ed., *Daedalus* (Summer 1978), p. 135.

[3] Anton F. J. Thibaut, *On Purity in Music,* W. H. Gladstone, trans. (London, 1877), p. 67.

Victor Hugo observes that whatever is systematic becomes "false, trivial and conventional"; and he condemns "petty conventional rules." [4]

According to Franz Liszt, Chopin "did violence to the peculiar nature of his genius when he endeavored to subject it to rules, to classifications and to regulations not of his own making . . . ." [5]

And Wagner writes that "The most perfect form of art . . . is that wherein all vestiges of conventionality are completely removed from the drama as well as from the music." [6]

Ideologically, the conventions of syntax and form — common cadential patterns and harmonic progressions, and familiar melodic or formal schemata — were anathema to Romantic composers. (A single speculation here speaks volumes: namely, one can scarcely imagine Berlioz, Wagner, or Mahler constructing dice games for the "composition" of music — as C.P.E. Bach, Haydn, and Mozart did!) Yet from a practical point of view, those who composed tonal music could no more dispense with the norms of grammar, syntax, and form than could poets and novelists. Such conventions were, after all, their "native language" — the way in which they had learned to "hear" and to comprehend the relationships among sounds.

The problems involved in reconciling the ideological rejection of conventions with the practical need for them were intensified by another dilemma. Two of the prime values of Romanticism were originality and individuality. Thus Liszt tells — and his view is thoroughly "Romantic" — that "the merit of perfecting a process can never equal the merit of inventing it";[7] while according to the musicologist Leon Plantinga, Schumann believed the characteris-

---

[4] "Preface to *Cromwell*," in *European Theories of the Drama*, B. H. Clark, ed. (New York, 1965), pp. 357 and 363.

[5] *The Life of Chopin*, J. Broadhouse, trans. (London, n.d.), p. 13.

[6] *Sämtliche Schriften und Dichtungen* (IX/112); quoted in Jack M. Stein, *Richard Wagner and the Synthesis of the Arts* (Westport, Conn., 1973), p. 167.

[7] *The Life of Chopin*, p. 139.

tics of Romantic music to be "an emphasis on originality rather than the normative." [8] But the existence of "originality" and the expression of individuality are invariably dependent upon — are defined and comprehended in terms of — existing norms of behavior, whether in life or in art. (Appropriately, the distinctive dress and demeanor of some of the artists of the period seems striking evidence that the delineation of individuality depends upon deviation from established norms and conventions.) Since especially for Romanticism, originality and individuality are virtually inseparable, I will treat them as more or less interchangeable notions.

The valuing of originality and individuality is correlative to the denigration and repudiation of convention because conventions, by definition, belong not to any individual, but to the compositional community. More important still, the repudiation of convention was, as I have suggested, a result of deep doubts about *all* social authority. For all authority — the state, the church, the community — seemed based upon apparently artificial rules and regulations. The only legitimate authority was the "natural authority" of the individual — preferably that of the inspired, but naïve, genius. The personal insight of the individual takes precedence over the shared norms of convention. The new "psychological man" of Romanticism was concerned not with social values and goals as much as with the realization of the potential latent in the individual ego. Thus Freud—one of the late-late Romantics— transforms the Oedipus story from one concerned with social morality and authority into one concerned with the inner development of the individual ego. As Philip Rieff so neatly puts it: "Oedipus Rex becomes Oedipus complex" [9] — which is the fate of every man.

[8] *Schumann as Critic* (New Haven, 1967), p. 108.

[9] *Freud: The Mind of the Moralist* (Chicago, 1979), p. 354.

It is interesting that both the type of change that occurred during the nineteenth century and its considerable force can be attributed to the claims of musical conventions on the one hand, and to those of the ideology of Romanticism on the other. The situation seems somewhat as follows. Because the constraints of tonality were indispensable for the organization of music, for the expression of feeling, and for the delineation of individuality, the kinds of innovation possible were quite limited. Changes were almost necessarily matters of degree—that is, what I have called "trended changes." [10] The ideological valuing of originality, however, put a premium on the invention and use of novelty. The result was evidently something comparable to what political scientists call "outbidding." That is, if a composer (or a group of composers) employed some musical means — say, an unusual harmony — in a relatively modest way, subsequent composers who wanted to use the same relationship were virtually compelled, in order to affirm their individuality, to increase the prevalence or the intensity of the means.

Even within the constraints of tonality, however, a multitude of alternatives were available or could have been devised.[11] Many of those actually chosen by composers can be interpreted and understood in terms of the model most favored by Romanticism: namely, that of the living, developing organism. Here is August Wilhelm Schlegel's characterization of two kinds of art:

> Form is mechanical when it is imparted to any material through an external force, merely as an accidental addition, without reference to its character. . . . Organic form, on the contrary, is innate; it unfolds itself from within, and reaches its deter-

[10] I have discussed the distinctions among different kinds of change in *Music, the Arts, and Ideas* (Chicago, 1967), pp. 99–101.

[11] One of the strategies devised to mediate between the antipathy toward, and the need for, conventions was the *disguise* of convention. This strategy is discussed in my "Exploiting Limits: Creation, Archetypes and Change," *Daedalus* (Spring 1980), pp. 177–205.

mination simultaneously with the fullest development of the seed. . . . In the fine arts, just as in the province of nature — the supreme artist — all genuine forms are organic.[12]

Although many of its tenets had been present in Western thought since ancient Greece, organicism was "politicized" and received its most forceful and thoroughgoing formulation as part of the ideology of Romanticism.[13] Organicism was crucial for the history of music; it furnished its central metaphors. The influence of organicism was so profound and persuasive that it has persisted, with occasional and minor remissions, throughout the twentieth century — not only in such "high-culture" manifestations as formalism, abstract painting, and avant-garde music, but in more mundane realms such as organic food and the back-to-nature subculture.

Despite its long history, the organic model had *not* been the main basis for conceptualizing musical relationships during the preceding century. Rather, as Leonard Ratner has shown us, language had been the favored model.[14] Musical structure was described in terms of phrases, sentences, and periods; expression, in terms of rhetoric and characteristic figures; and unity was understood to be a function of both expression and tonal structure. As was the case with language, grammar and syntax, rhetoric and gestural expression, and even formal organization seemed learned and conventional. And, as with language, such learned typologies, rules, and procedures tended to be associated with lineage, class, and hierarchic authority. Thus the shift from the language model to the organic model constitutes both a symptom and a conse-

[12] *On Dramatic Art and Literature*; quoted in M. L. Abrams, *The Mirror and the Lamp* (London, 1976), p. 213.

[13] For a discussion of the influence of organicism on music theory, see Ruth A. Solie, "The Living Work: Organicism and Musical Analysis," *19th-Century Music* 4, no. 2 (Fall 1980), pp. 147–56.

[14] "Eighteenth-Century Theories of Musical Period Structure," *Musical Quarterly* 42 (1956), pp. 439–54.

quence of the repudiation of convention and class. To exaggerate
somewhat: the language model represents a prizing of societal
constraints; the organic model celebrates the felicities of natural
constraints.

The core metaphor of organicism likens a work of art to a
living thing — usually a flowering plant — whose germination,
growth, and coherence result, in Coleridge's words, from "an antecedent Power or Principle in the Seed." [15] Just as a seed gives rise
to the diverse parts of a plant (to roots and stems, leaves and
flowers), so in a composition the diverse themes, harmonic relationships, etc., are taken to be manifestations of a single basic
principle — be it a melodic motive, a fundamental chord, a rhythmic germ, or even a sonority. That this metaphor was part of the
thinking of composers, as well as aestheticians, is evident in Wagner's account of the composition of *The Flying Dutchman* and,
more particularly, of Senta's second-act ballad.

> . . . in this piece I unwittingly *planted the thematic seed* of all
> the music of the opera. . . . When I came eventually to the
> composition, the thematic image I had already conceived quite
> involuntarily spread over the entire drama in a complete un-
> broken web; all that was left for me to do was to allow the
> various *thematic germs* contained in the ballad *to develop to
> the full, each in its own direction.* . . .[16]

As Wagner's description indicates, organic growth is gradual. Nor
is the way that the seed develops arbitrary or capricious; rather the
process of growth is determined by the presence of some underlying principle.

In addition to being gradual, organic processes were conceived
as being goal-directed. The goal, as Lovejoy has shown, was

---

15 *Aids to Reflection*; quoted in Abrams, *The Mirror and the Lamp*, p. 271.

16 *A Communication to my Friends*; quoted in Carl Dahlhaus, *Richard Wagner's
Music Dramas*, Mary Whittall, trans. (Cambridge, 1979), p. 18.

emergent self-realization on all levels of the natural order.[17] Instead of a fixed hierarchy of kinds and classes, established once and for all by God's creation, there is a continuing process in which the innate potential of nature is realized gradually. (The political implications of this shift are unmistakable.) The goal of the individual, too, is self-realization. And it is from this point of view that Schumann criticizes Chopin:

> Now Chopin could publish everything anonymously; everyone would recognize him anyway. In this there is both praise and blame — praise for his talent, blame for his effort. . . . Always new and inventive in externals, in the shape of his compositions, in his special instrumental effects, yet he remains in essence the same. Because of this we fear he will never achieve a higher level than he has already reached. . . . With his abilities he could have achieved far more, influencing the progress of our art as a whole.[18]

In short, to realize oneself is to become differentiated from others — to be original — and to continue such "progress." And the almost mystic valuing of self-realization (and its counterpart self-expression) in our own culture is evidence, once again, of the continued power of Romantic ideology.

But complete self-realization is an unachievable goal. For Romanticism, man's true nature is one of restless striving after a perfection that can never be his. Just as the world is forever in a state of Becoming, so man is — and so his art should be. What Friederich van Schlegel says of poetry holds for the other arts as well:

> . . . Romantic poetry is constantly developing. That in fact is its true nature; it can forever only *become*, it can never achieve definitive form. . . . Its overriding principle is that the poet's fantasy is subject to no agreed principles. Romantic poetry is

[17] Arthur O. Lovejoy, *The Great Chain of Being* (New York, 1960), ch. 9.

[18] Quoted in Leon Plantinga, *Schumann as Critic*, p. 321.

the only poetry that is more than a poetic genre. It is, so to speak, the very art of poetry itself. Indeed, in a certain sense, all poetry is — or should be — romantic.[19]

The emphasis on *becoming* — on continuous growth and unfolding — finds musical expression not only in the sense of "yearning" associated with unfulfilled striving, but also in a valuing of open forms and unrealized implications.

I shall consider the nature of form in Romantic music toward the end of this essay. But first I shall discuss some of the ways in which the values connected with organicism were translated into smaller-scale compositional strategies. More specifically, I shall focus on Romantic melody, not only because other facets of Romantic music have been much more extensively discussed, but because both composers and theorists of the period considered melody to be the heart and soul of musical expression. In the words of Schopenhauer, perhaps the philosopher who best represented Romantic thinking about music:

> . . . in melody . . . which dominates the whole and progresses freely in a single uninterrupted, coherent and meaningful idea from start to finish, I recognize the highest stage of the objectification of the Will, the conscious life and strife of man. . . . [Melody] tells the story of the Will as illuminated by self-awareness. . . . But melody expresses still more: it reveals the Will's secret history, portrays its every movement, its every endeavor, everything that reason comprehends under the broad pejorative concept of emotion, being incapable of further abstraction.[20]

Melody receives prime place in the pantheon of musical parameters because it was consonant with the ideals most highly prized by the ideology of Romanticism. Harmony and counterpoint could

---

[19] *Kritische Schriften*; excerpted in P. le Huray and J. Day, *Music and Aesthetics in the Eighteenth and Early-Nineteenth Centuries* (Cambridge, 1981), pp. 246–47.

[20] *Die Welt als Wille und Vorstellung*; excerpted in le Huray and Day, *Music and Aesthetics*, p. 327.

be taught and learned — their rules could be found in treatises; forms could be classified and analyzed into hierarchies of parts and subparts. But, to quote Schopenhauer once again, "The composition of melody . . . is the work of genius, whose action . . . lies far from all reflection and conscious intention, and may be called inspiration." [21]

II

Many of the values of organicism — gradual growth and emergence, goal-directed motion, openness and continual becoming — are realized in a strategy that I call "stretching." Stretching is also, and importantly, related to other values of Romanticism — especially to the reliance upon natural, as opposed to conventional, means. For stretching is one way of reconciling the claims of nature with those of intense expression.

Basically, melodic stretching involves an increase either in the size of a melodic interval or in the length of a rhythmic unit in relation to a *standard* previously established in the particular piece. The difference between Classic and Romantic music is one of emphasis. Composers of the Classic period wrote stretch melodies, but they did so less often than did composers in the nineteenth century. Even more important, the use made of stretching tends to change. I will illustrate this with an example from the Classic period and with several from the Romantic period.

The transition passage from the first movement of Mozart's String Quintet in G Minor (K. 516) contains a clear example of stretching (Example 1). A motive that begins with a skip (or gap), which establishes the *standard*, occurs twice. Then at the start of the second part of the phrase-group (m. 32), the skip is stretched to a larger interval and the duration of the accented tone is doubled. The second phrase-group (mm. 34–39) begins like the first, but its second part is stretched in time (see the "phrase

[21] Ibid.

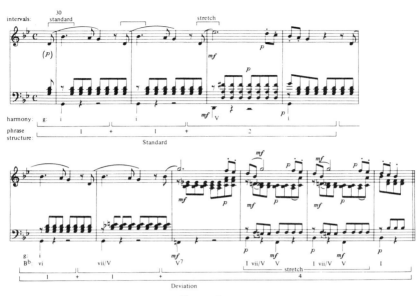

Example 1

structure" analysis below Example 1), becoming twice as long as it was before (four measures instead of two).

The expressive tension of these stretches needs no comment. As is usually the case, the upper note of the stretched interval is a discordant, accented nonharmonic tone called an appoggiatura. The discordance, calling for resolution, produces a sense of goal-directed motion — motion that will create a sense of relative completeness by presenting the tones omitted by the skip. What needs to be noticed is that the stretching in this passage is part of a syntactic process: that is, the stretching is part of a change of key (a modulatory, harmonic process) and by the end of the passage the new key (B♭) is established.

In the famous melody of Schumann's "Träumerei," however, stretching has no syntactic function. Rather it essentially serves the end of expression. The music consists of two phrases (Example 2). The second begins like the first and could have continued

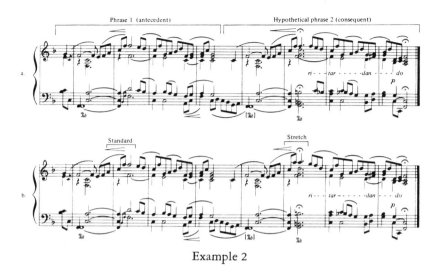

Example 2

like the first, except for the closing cadence. That is, the melody *might* have been as shown in Example 2a.

Instead of this repetition, for the second half of the period, Schumann stretches the interval at the end of the first melodic gesture (Example 2b). The expressive tension of the stretch is heightened both by the harmony (the high note is a discord, where in the first phrase it was a concord) and by the fact that the resolution of this discord is delayed by a fermata ($\curvearrowright$), lengthening the high note. These intensifications are, however, largely local. The basic harmonic relationships of the passage are not significantly affected by the size of the skip. Instead, what the stretch does — in addition to heightening expressive tension — is to give the melody a point of culmination; and such "high points" are, as we shall see, very characteristic of Romantic form. The close of the period is, in typical Romantic fashion, characterized by *abatement*[22] — a gradual cessation of activity and tension, a dying-away

---

[22] I have borrowed the term "abatement" from Robert G. Hopkins. See his "Secondary Parameters and Closure in the Symphonies of Gustav Mahler" (Ph.D. diss., University of Pennsylvania, 1983), p. 3f. and *passim*.

created by descending pitches, softer dynamics, and a slowing down ("ritardando") to the final note, which is prolonged by a fermata.

As the Mozart and Schumann examples suggest, melodic stretching usually occurs as an aspect of what I call a gap-fill schema.[23] The schema has two parts. In the first, and generally shorter part, a skip (almost always rising) creates an incompleteness: the gap. In the second part, or fill, the notes skipped over in the first part are presented in more or less linear scale-like order. Especially in stretch melodies it is typical that the top note of the gap is an appoggiatura — that is, a tensive discord that gives direction and impetus to the ensuing fill.

Stretching is a favored strategy of nineteenth-century composers not only because of its expressive power, but also because that power arises from a direct comparison that is not dependent upon syntactic convention. That is, stretching is a "natural" kind of relationship. And it seems obvious that the closer in time the patterns being compared are to one another, the more patent and effective modifications, such as stretching, will be. For this reason, as the nineteenth century moves on, and as composers choose weaker syntactic constraints, the *standard* pattern and the *stretch* are directly juxtaposed instead of being separated by intervening material, as in Schumann's melody. Furthermore, I suspect that there is a tendency for both the relative frequency of stretch melodies and the size of the stretches to increase.

These traits are evident in many of the melodies of the Romantic period. One well-known passage will serve as illustration. It is the "Kiss" theme from Verdi's *Otello* (Example 3). Verdi's melody is intense. This is not only the result of melodic relationships, but also of harmonic ones which create an atmosphere of ambiguity and instability. The ambience of tension is both

---

[23] The nature of "gap-fill" melodies is discussed in my *Explaining Music: Essays and Explorations* (Berkeley, 1973), pp. 145–57.

heightened and characterized by the manifest, yet tender, ardor of the melody. For the stretching that expresses desire is compounded: not only does the second presentation of the "Kiss motive stretch the interval of the first (the standard), but the third presentation of the motive stretches the preceding one — reaching the upper octave ($C^\sharp$), which serves to signify completion of the rising motion. Contributing to this tension is the prevalence of appoggiaturas, which occur on the first beat of each measure.

The prevalence of appoggiaturas in the music of Romanticism can scarcely be exaggerated. And it can readily be related to the ideology of Romanticism. To the extent that sonic tension and melodic tendency are generated by discord, the expressive and processive power of appoggiaturas is "natural" — that is, independent of explicitly syntactic convention. The sense of downward

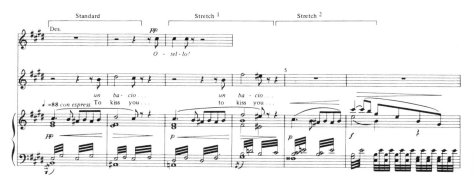

Example 3

pull toward a note of greater concordance gives such figures a strong affective character — a character that, generally speaking, becomes more pronounced as the relative duration of appoggiaturas increases over the course of the nineteenth century. From a rhythmic point of view, appoggiaturas create mobile, on-going rhythms that are associated with the Romantic valuing of openness, becoming, and continual growth. Harmonically, extended appoggiaturas give rise to ambiguity by generating doubts about relative functional importance and, in so doing, they often obscure the nature of syntactic processes.

Though stretching is a strategy characteristic of much Romantic music, not all composers chose to use it. Indeed, two of the most important composers of the period, Wagner and Debussy, seem expressly to avoid it. But they do so for very different reasons.

Wagner's avoidance is, as I see it, related to the development and use of the leitmotive as a narrative and symbolic device. Leitmotives are musical ideas that have referential, narrative significance — symbolizing people, concepts, and objects.[24] Because of their referential role, leitmotives must be readily recognizable in a variety of musical and dramatic contexts. And to be recognizable, they must be relatively constant. Stretching is avoided, I suggest, because it tends to disturb such constancy.

I am not asserting that melodic stretching never occurs in Wagner's music. But I suspect that when it does, it is in connection with lyric passages; for instance, there are unequivocal stretches in the "Prize Song" from *Die Meistersinger*. Nor do I wish to imply that Wagner did not employ the kinds of schemata typical of Romantic music. Gap-fill melodies, for instance, abound in his works — especially at points of fervent lyricism, as in Example 4,

---

[24] As far as I can see, the tendency of contemporary scholars to denigrate the semantic function of leitmotives is simply continuing evidence of formalist snobbery. Serious criticism of Wagner's music must concern itself with the relationship between form and process on the one hand and symbolic/semantic function on the other.

Example 4

a passage from the first act of *Die Walküre*. Though the passage consists of a succession — a rising sequence — of octave gaps, there are no stretched intervals. Nevertheless, the music is strongly goal-directed, not only in melodic plan (emphasized, again, by strong appoggiaturas), but also in harmony which moves to a prolonged dominant chord.

Debussy, too, chooses motivic constancy rather than stretching. He does so, however, not because his motives have a semantic function, but in order to emphasize the sensuous qualities of sound per se. Only by expressly weakening the processive, goal-directed aspects of experience can we be forced, as it were, to attend primarily to the qualities of sense experience — to the timbre of a particular instrument, the sound of a specific harmony, and so on.[25] For this reason, Debussy avoids not only stretching but other relationships that are patently processive as well. In his music there are few clearly syntactic harmonic progressions, such as that from the subdominant to the dominant, and almost no goal-directed melodic schemata such as gap-fill patterns.

III

I now want to consider a broad and fundamental difference in the kinds of schemata that tend to be chosen by eighteenth- versus

---

[25] For further discussion of this point see my *Music, the Arts, and Ideas*, p. 73f.

nineteenth-century composers. This difference corresponds in many respects to the distinction that psychologists have made between scripts and plans, and I shall use their terminology. The changing-note schema (to be discussed shortly) and the gap-fill patterning already described will serve to exemplify the distinction between scripts and plans.[26] According to Roger Schank and Robert Abelson, "A script is a structure . . . made up of slots and requirements about what can fill those slots. The structure is an interconnected whole, and what is in one slot affects what can be in another." [27] Melodies based on the changing-note schema fill this prescription. That schema, and others like it, stipulate specific melodic, harmonic, and formal possibilities and probabilities. In other words, they are inextricably linked to syntactic constraints. Melodies based on the gap-fill schema, on the other hand, involve more general relationships. Very little is stipulated about particular pitches, harmonies, and formal relationships. Any skip-pattern can act as a gap, while a wide variety of different, but more or less conjunct, pitch successions can function as a fill — and harmony and form will vary accordingly. Schemata of this sort are akin to plans. As described by Schank and Abelson, plans are repositories "for general information that will connect events that cannot be connected by use of an available script. . . . A plan explains how a given state or event was prerequisite for, or derived from, another state or event." [28]

This distinction suggests a broad hypothesis that warrants more careful confirmation than can be attempted here. The hy-

---

[26] Changing-note melodies are discussed in my *Explaining Music*, pp. 191–96, and in Burton Rosner and Leonard B. Meyer, "Melodic Processes and the Perception of Music," in Diana Deutsch, ed., *The Psychology of Music* (New York, 1982), pp. 317–41.

[27] *Scripts, Plans, Goals and Understanding: An Inquiry into Human Knowledge Structures* (Hillsdale, N.J., 1977), p. 41. I am grateful to Robert Gjerdingen for calling this distinction and the work of Schank and Abelson to my attention.

[28] Ibid., pp. 70 and 77.

pothesis is this: music of the Classic period is dominated by syntactic scripts; music of the Romantic period, on the other hand, tends to favor the use of general plans. To illustrate this point, I shall begin by describing the shift from the use of changing-note melodies, which are script-based, to what have been called "axial" melodies, which are less stipulative — that is, more plan-like.[29] Again, it is important to recognize that the shift being considered is a matter of emphasis.

The changing-note schema can occur on different steps of the scale. The one I shall discuss is on the third of the scale. It is defined by the following features: a melodic pattern that begins on the third of the scale, moves a step above and a step below the third of the scale, and then returns to the third; a harmonic progression from the tonic (I) to the dominant (V), and then back from the dominant to the tonic; and a balanced formal structure composed of two similar parts (A-A'). Two unadorned realizations will illustrate this schema. The first is from the Finale of Act II of Mozart's *Marriage of Figaro* (Example 5a) ; the second is the closing theme of the last movement of Schubert's Octet in F Major, Opus 166 (Example 5b). In both instances the successive pitches of the melody (3-4//2-3, in the Mozart; and 3-2//4-3, in the Schubert) fill their assigned slots; the harmonic progression (I-V//V-I) is as stipulated; and the formal plan (A-A') complies with the requirements of the script.

The beginning of the second key-area tune from the first movement of Schubert's String Quintet in C Major (Opus 163) is much less script-like (Example 6). Though the pitches (3-4//2-3) characteristic of the schema are present, harmony combines with rhythm and phrase structure to obscure formal parallelism. Instead of a script, consisting of a statement and a balanced response, the effect is that of a central tone (the third of the scale over tonic

---

[29] The term "axial" is borrowed from Eugene Narmour, *Beyond Schenkerism* (Chicago, 1977), p. 22f. I have discussed axial patterns in *Explaining Music,* pp. 183–91.

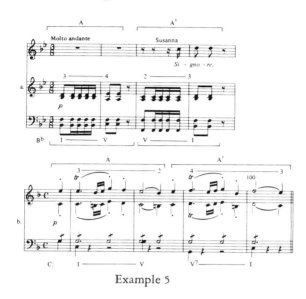

Example 5

harmony) which functions as an axis around which upper and lower neighboring tones revolve and toward which they tend to gravitate. Put differently: as the script stipulations of the changing-note schema become partially weakened, the general axial plan — that is, move away from and return to a central tone — becomes relatively more important.

Two more examples will serve to emphasize the points being made. Both the lyric melody from Liszt's *Les Preludes* (Exam-

Example 6

ple 7a) and the somber theme that opens the slow movement of
Brahms' Fourth Symphony (Example 7b) are plainly axial —
moving around, and returning to, a focal center, without necessary reference to a clear syntactic script. And, after less than decisive closure, both themes repeat their axial patterns a major third
higher (on G$\sharp$).

Changing-note melodies continued to be written throughout
the nineteenth century, though usually disguised in some way. But
the proportion of axial melodies increased dramatically. Composers chose them because they were consonant with the ideas of
Romanticism. For instance, the generally weak closure of axial
patterns accords with the Romantic valuing of the continuousness
of open forms. Absence of strong syntactic closure also facilitated
the composition of large musical structures; and magnitude was
prized by Romantics as an aspect of the sublime. That is, because
axial patterns are open, they can easily be repeated either at the
same or a different pitch-level. In this way, as in Liszt's *Les Preludes*, four measures could be extended to sixteen — and perhaps
even more. (For composers who chose to rely upon convention
as little as possible and, consequently, had to make many time-

Example 7

consuming compositional choices, such economy was not a trivial
consideration.)

Most important of all, axial melodies are understandable in the
absence of syntactic conventions. A comparison of the constraints
governing axial and changing-note melodies will help to make this
clear. In axial melodies, the prime process generating tonal tension is that of departure from a central pitch, followed by the
satisfaction of return to that pitch. Our experience of this can be
attributed to innate (i.e., natural) cognitive proclivities. Changing-
note melodies also depart from and return to a central tone. But
when *they* do so, the process is to a considerable extent understood
as being governed by the learned constraints of tonal syntax. Put
differently: a listener who understood nothing of tonality would
perceive a changing-note melody as being axial. In short, in
changing-note melodies nurture dominates nature, while in axial
melodies it is the other way around.

A comparable shift in emphasis characterizes the history of
gap-fill melodies. Although the schema is plan-like, eighteenth-
century realizations of it tend to be dominated by syntactic scripts
such as antecedent-consequent relationships. That is, each phrase
of the melody contains a gap that is followed by a fill; but the
first phrase reaches only partial closure (normally on some note of
the dominant triad), while the second reaches greater closure (on
one of the tones of the tonic triad). In other words, the phrase

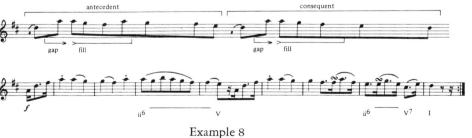

Example 8

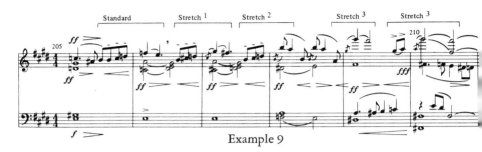

Example 9

relationships are stipulated by a script. For instance, and typically in eighteenth-century music, both the antecedent and consequent phrases of the Minuetto of Mozart's Flute Quartet in A (Example 8) begin with a gap pattern. But instead of returning to the tonic, the first fill ends with a half cadence (V) just before reaching the tonic. The syntactic script, as it were, prevents the gap-fill plan from reaching completion. Then, in the second phrase, the fill is complete and is coordinate with syntactic closure.

In the music of Romanticism, script constraints tend to be attenuated and, late in the period, virtually disappear. Often, as though to compensate for the weakening of syntactic relationships, the generating force of an initial gap is reinforced through re-iteration. A melody from the third movement of Mahler's Fourth Symphony provides a clear instance of gap reiteration coupled with forceful melodic stretching (Example 9). Though the nature of the plan is emphatic and unequivocal, the syntactic goal seems ambiguous until the very end. Instead of resolving, the dominant harmony is dissipated when the highest note is not only repeated but prolonged.

Despite the intensity of the successively stretched gaps and discordant appoggiaturas, the implied fill does not follow until some hundred measures later.[30] There, following a monumental affirmation of the local tonic (mm. 315–320), the melody gradually de-

[30] Because of its length, no example is given. The reader is asked to consult Mahler's score.

scends through a fill (mm. 320–353) — but one that is only weakly syntactic because it first avoids the leading-tone of the scale and then the fourth step of the scale. The whole end of the movement consists of a process of gradual subsidence in which the music dies away without decisive melodic, rhythmic or harmonic closure. As the final harmony, the dominant, makes evident, the end is open — leading to the last movement of the Symphony.

Taken by itself, this final fill seems a somewhat feeble response to the forceful tensions of the many stretched intervals and discordant appoggiaturas that went before. Moreover, though the nature of the gap-fill schema is not in doubt, the myriad different gaps — none adequately or proximately filled — makes it difficult to know which, if any, is the gap that establishes criteria for a satisfactory fill and, consequently, what, if anything, would constitute an adequate fill. Nevertheless, the end seems satisfying. For tension has been more than merely dissipated in subsidence — the gradual dying-away. Particular fills, specific resolutions are unnecessary, I believe, because the magnitude and power of the apotheosis-like affirmation serve to absolve prior implicative and syntactic obligations. That is, the unrealized implications of melodic and harmonic relationships, the unresolved tensions of syntactic processes, and the ambiguous formal juxtapositions are absorbed or dissolved through the sheer intensity of what I call the statistical climax.

IV

Reference to apotheosis, statistical climax, and subsidence — all terms that will be explained shortly — brings me to the final topic to be discussed: namely, musical form.[31] Once again, the differences between Classic and Romantic music, though matters of emphasis, are clear. Classic music tends to employ script-

---

[31] Many of the matters considered in this section are discussed in somewhat greater detail in two earlier articles: "Toward a Theory of Style," in Berel Lang, ed., *The Concept of Style* (Philadelphia, 1979), pp. 3–44, and "Exploiting Limits."

dominated forms; Romantic music tends to employ plan-dominated ones. To understand the relationship between the ideology of Romanticism and the shift from script- to plan-domination, it is necessary to consider some of the differences between the primary and secondary parameters of music.

Melody, harmony, and rhythm are understood to be the primary parameters of music because they are governed by syntactic constraints — constraints, that is, which stipulate relationships of relative mobility, stability, and closure. The primary parameters give rise to what I call *syntactic form*, and important points of structural articulation — turning points in the form — are, accordingly, called *syntactic climaxes*. Because they can create clear closure, the primary parameters make hierarchic structures possible. Indeed, a musical form is usually analyzed in terms of the closural strengths of its several parts. Such analyses in turn lead to the classification of form based upon part/whole relationships. Last, because the parts of any hierarchy have a degree of autonomy, they (as well as the whole work) can be thought of as possessing the actuality of *being* rather than only the potentiality of *becoming*. It should be evident by now that these characteristics of syntactic form — dependence upon learned convention, the existence of hierarchies, the classification of more or less fixed types, and the actuality of being — were scarcely values of Romanticism.

Dynamics, timbre, rates of activity, pitch-frequency, concord and discord, and so on are understood to be secondary parameters. Because they do not stipulate relationships of relative mobility, stability, and closure, these parameters do not give rise to syntax. Instead of stipulative relationships such as leading-tone to tonic, subdominant to dominant, upbeat to downbeat, antecedent/consequent, the relationships created by secondary parameters involve changes in relative amount along an unsegmented continuum: for instance, faster or slower pitch-frequency, louder or softer dynamics, higher or lower rates of activity, etc.

Because such differences are quantitative, I call both the secondary parameters and the forms to which they give rise, *statistical*. The basic paradigm for statistical form is what Leonard Ratner has called the "dynamic curve" — a succession of cumulative, wave-like shapes in which the music builds to a highpoint, subsides somewhat, and builds again, until, toward the end of the work, the point of highest intensity is reached.[32] After that, there is a gradual subsidence toward cessation and silence. The highpoints in such dynamic curves are *statistical climaxes*.

The ability of secondary parameters to shape musical experience is less dependent upon learned constraints and conventions. In this sense their effects are "natural" rather than artificial, and their increased importance is consonant with the beliefs and attitudes of Romanticism. A passage consisting of gradually rising pitches, louder dynamics, faster rates of motion, a greater number of parts, and heightened degrees of discord will produce tension and excitement. Such *intensifying* passages lead to statistical climaxes. Passages of the opposite sort — consisting of descending pitches, slower rates of motion, softer dynamics, and so on — will, of course, reduce tension, leading to relaxation and repose. Such *abating* processes lead to cessation.

The music of the past century and a half abounds with examples of statistical form. On a small scale, the prevalence of the plan affected many of the excerpts considered earlier in the lecture — Schumann's "Träumerei," the "Kiss" theme from Verdi's *Otello*, the sequential passage from Wagner's *Die Walküre*, and the highpoint and abatement from Mahler's Fourth Symphony. My illustration of larger-scale statistical form — perhaps the most famous exemplification of all — will be the last part of Isolde's "Liebestod" from Wagner's *Tristan und Isolde*.[33]

[32] *Music: The Listener's Art* (New York, 1966), pp. 314–16.

[33] Because of its length, the music is not given; the passage referred to begins with the words "in mich dringet, auf sich schwinget . . ." and goes to the end of the opera.

Little needs to be said about the first part of the "Liebestod's" typically three-stage form: the gradually rising wave-like surges of intensification seem to strive toward some unattainable goal. In Liszt's words, what is expressed is "all that relates to the inaccessible depths of imperishable desires and longing for the infinite."[34] The statistical climax — here a briefly sustained highpoint[35] — is related to an important value of Romanticism: that is, the expression of the sublime. As Peter Lichtenthal wrote in his Dictionary of 1826,

> Pleasure in the sublime is distinguished from pleasure in the beautiful, in that whereas the beautiful relates to the *form* of things, that is to say to their *quality*, the sublime is a matter of their *size*, or *quantity* and may be found in objects devoid of form, such as enormous masses of rock. . . . So the sublime is that which, by its immeasurable grandeur, stimulates the action of reason increasing its vital senses. Indeed, as Kant and Schiller have said, the sublime comprises the infinite which terrifies the senses and the imagination beyond the powers of comprehension. . . .[36]

It should be obvious that the distinction between syntactic form (stipulated by the primary parameters) and statistical form (fostered by secondary parameters) corresponds closely to the distinction between the beautiful and the sublime — a distinction that was part of the scuttlebutt of Romanticism.

The abating processes that follow the statistical highpoint of the "Liebestod" lead to cessation, but not to definitive closure.[37] Because the relationships created by secondary parameters involve incremental changes along a continuum, they establish states of

---

[34] Preface to the *Album d'un voyageur*; excerpted in le Huray and Day, *Music and Aesthetics*, p. 537.

[35] During the words "Welt Atems wehen dem All . . . ."

[36] *Dizionario e Bibliografia della Musica*; excerpted in le Huray and Day, *Music and Aesthetics*, p. 372.

[37] Beginning with the words "ertrinken, versinken . . . ."

relative, rather than stipulative, tension and repose. When, for example, does a *diminuendo*—a gradual softening of dynamics— reach closure? When does a gradual slowing of rate of motion do so? The answer is *never*. Secondary parameters cannot create definitive closure. They can only cease or die away into nothing- ness. And precisely because they cannot close, the gradual abate- ment of the secondary parameters suggests the eternal continuous- ness of Becoming.

The openness of the abatement of secondary parameters is sup- ported by harmonic relationships — relationships which suggest that Wagner deliberately avoided both conventional and definitive closure. The sustained highpoint of the "Liebestod" occurs over a forceful dominant-seventh chord. But instead of leading to cus- tomary closure on the tonic, the seventh chord moves — resolves is too strong a word — to the subdominant. And it is subdominant harmony that leads, somewhat inconclusively, to the softly sus- tained tonic chord at the end.

The abatement that ends the "Liebestod" not only signifies musical cessation — the end of the opera as well as the aria — but also relevant and important extramusical ideas: ideas associ- ated with the deaths of Tristan and Isolde, with eternal Becoming, and with the redemption of the lovers. The redemption is symbol- ized both by the religious "overtones" of the "Amen," or plagal, cadence and by the heavenly height of the sustained violins and woodwinds.

Statistical form, such as that illustrated by the "Liebestod," is continuous. The ideal, consonant with the notions of organicism, is one of gradual, seamless unfolding — a process of natural and necessary growth that contrasts sharply with the presumably arti- ficial and arbitrary part/whole hierarchies characteristic of syn- tactic form. However striking they may *appear* to be, differences and contrasts, as well as part/whole relationships, are regarded as accidental, illusory manifestations of a single process or principle that governs the succession of patterns in the work. Moreover, in the Romantic view the process or principle that imparts meaning and unity to the composition almost invariably lies concealed beneath the trappings and suits of diversity. Such underlying principles have a tendency to become reified — to be thought of as the "real" stuff of works of art, while the sights, sounds, and smells of the world are considered to be but second-order happenstance. From this point of view, organicism is Platonism in biological clothing.

The prevalence of statistical form and the correlative increase in the importance of secondary parameters had significant consequences for music composition and theory in the nineteenth century. Because secondary parameters cannot create decisive closure, they cannot give rise to clearly articulated hierarchic structures. In the absence of hierarchy, and in the absence of belief in the efficacy of convention which normalizes the presence of contrast and disparity, the basis of musical unity becomes a pressing problem. That is, smaller parts cannot be subsumed within larger ones; as a result, contrasting harmonies and conflicting melodies confront one another directly in the confined space of foreground juxtaposition. How do patently different events, disparate gestures, contrasts of expression form coherent wholes? The persistent — almost obsessive — preoccupation in music theory and aesthetics generally, with the nature and sources of unity is testimony to the power of the denigration of convention and the decline in hierarchic structuring.

Of the various means employed to unify compositions perhaps the most important and pervasive was that of thematic transformation. Reflecting the power and prevalence of the organic model, thematic transformation involved the derivation of all the patterns and relationships of a composition from a single motivic cell. Carl Czerny's description of Beethoven's Third Piano Concerto is representative of this conception of unity. Writing around 1828, he observes that, following the first tutti, "all other passages are drawn from the principal theme, by which means the composition obtains that characteristic *unity* by which it is so highly distinguished." [38] And theorist Peter Lichtenthal, writing around the same time, asserts that "Amongst the works of the great masters may be found innumerable pieces that are built on a single motif. What marvellous unity there is in the structure of these compositions." [39]

Observe that, according to this conception, unity is independent of convention, tonal syntax, and learning. Instead, it arises out of similarity relationships among musical patterns. If such similarities are at times difficult to discern, this is because the process of organic growth and transformation that generates a surface diversity often conceals the underlying, generating musical cell or principle. That this kind of organic unity is independent of conventional constraints is evident in the fact that it constitutes the basis for much non-tonal contemporary music — especially serialism. That the ideology of Romanticism which spawned such views of unity is still very much with us is evident not only in the oppressive prevalence of "deep structures"—whether those of Chomskian linguistics, Freudian psychology, or Schenkerian music theory — but also in the writings of music theorists and composers. Here is what one of the most influential serial composers, Anton Webern, had to say about Bach's *Art of Fugue*:

> All these fugues are created from one single theme, which is constantly transformed. . . . What does all this mean: An effort towards an all-embracing unity. . . . So we see that this — our — kind of thought has been the ideal for composers of all periods. . . . To develop everything from a single principal idea! [40]

[38] *School of Practical Composition*, vol. I (London, 1848), p. 164.

[39] *Dizionario e Bibliografia della Musica*; excerpted in le Huray and Day, *Music and Aesthetics*, p. 374.

[40] Anton Webern, "Towards a New Music," *The Score*, no. 28 (January 1961), p. 30.

Thus we come to our own times; but not to the end of Romanticism. Both in practice and in theory its powerful presence is still pervasive — in the primitivism of popular music, in the statistical music of composers such as Xenakis, in the minimalism of Reich and Glass, and in the formalism of much music theory and much of music aesthetics. The consequences of Romanticism for the great tradition of Western art music have been ironic and paradoxical: for the repudiation of supposedly artificial conventions and arbitrary hierarchies in favor of presumably natural relationships not dependent upon learning has led to music which, far from being egalitarian and accessible, has proved to be elitist and academic. And this untoward outcome, I believe, poses an important — even profound — question about humankind: namely, whether it is our nature to be naïvely natural — without cultivated concepts and conventional constraints.

I must stop here, since the classic constraints of conventional lecture-time have been stretched to the limit. And it seems appropriate, given the concerns of this lecture, to end not with definitive closure, but with Romantic openness.[41]

[41] This essay owes an incalculable debt to the perceptive and cogent criticisms of my wife, Janet M. Levy.

Challenges to Neo-Darwinism and Their Meaning for a Revised View of Human Consciousness

STEPHEN JAY GOULD

THE TANNER LECTURES ON HUMAN VALUES

Delivered at
Clare Hall, Cambridge University

April 30 and May 1, 1984

STEPHEN JAY GOULD was born in New York City in 1941 and educated at Antioch College and Columbia University. He has taught at Harvard University since 1967, from 1973 as Professor of Geology and Curator of Invertebrate Paleontology in the Museum of Comparative Zoology, and since 1982 as Alexander Agassiz Professor of Zoology.

Professor Gould has received a number of academic medals and awards, the most recent of which are the Silver Medal of the Zoological Society of London (1984) and the Meritorious Service Award of the American Association of Systematics Collections (1984). Several of his books have been recognized with literary awards; most recently, *Hen's Teeth and Horse's Toes* received the Phi Beta Kappa book award in science. Dr. Gould is a member of the American Academy of Arts and Sciences and President of the Paleontological Society, and among his grants and fellowships is the MacArthur Foundation Prize Fellowship (1981–86).

I. Basic Premises of the Synthetic Theory

The odyssey of evolution in the history of ideas has been, in microcosm, much like the history of species, the macrocosm that it seeks to explain — peculiar, tortuous, unpredictable, complex, weighted down by past inheritances, and not moving in unilinear fashion toward any clear goal.

Darwin divided his life's work, explicitly and often, into two major goals: to demonstrate the fact that evolution had occurred, and to promote the theory of natural selection as its primary mechanism. In the first quest, his success was abundant, and he now lies in Westminster Abbey, at the feet of Isaac Newton, for this triumph. In the second, he made much less headway during his lifetime. By the close of the nineteenth century, natural selection was a strong contender in a crowded field of evolutionary theories, but it held no predominant position.

Darwinian concepts are now so canonical in evolutionary theory that students without historical perspective often assume it has been so since 1859. In fact, the triumph of natural selection as a centerpiece of evolutionary theory dates only to a major intellectual movement of the 1930s and 1940s, called by Julian Huxley (1942) the "modern synthesis." The synthesis validated natural selection as a powerful causal agent and raised it from a former status as one contender among many to a central position among mechanisms of change (the role assigned to natural selection later hardened to near exclusivity; see Gould, 1983). The modern synthesis is, essentially, the central logic of Darwin's argument updated by the genetic theory of variation and inheritance that he, perforce, lacked.

Ernst Mayr, leading architect and historian of the modern synthesis, offered this definition of its primary claims at a con-

ference that assembled all the leading originators (in Mayr and
Provine, 1980, p. 1):

> The term "evolutionary synthesis" was introduced by Julian
> Huxley . . . to designate the general acceptance of two con-
> clusions: gradual evolution can be explained in terms of small
> genetic changes ("mutations") and recombination, and the
> ordering of this genetic variation by natural selection; and the
> observed evolutionary phenomena, particularly macroevolu-
> tionary processes and speciation, can be explained in a manner
> that is consistent with the known genetic mechanisms.

Several major tenets may be distilled from this paragraph. I
shall select three as inspirations for major critiques of the hegemony of Neo-Darwinism. Each has significance for a revised view
of human consciousness and its evolutionary meaning.

1. *Chance and necessity.* Randomness and determinism occupy
separate and definite spheres in the central logic of Darwin's
theory. As Mayr states above, genetic variation arises by mutation
and recombination; it is then ordered by natural selection —
chance for the origin of the raw material of change, determination
for the selective incorporation of some of this variation into
altered organisms.

The central logic of Darwinism requires that natural selection
not merely operate, but that it be the creative force of evolutionary
change. Selection wins its role as a creative force because the
other component of evolutionary mechanics — the forces that produce the raw material of genetic variation — are random, in the
special sense of "not inherently directed toward adaptation." That
is, if local environments change and smaller organisms are now
at an advantage, genetic variation does not produce more small
individuals, thus imparting a direction to evolutionary change
from the level of variation itself. Variation continues to occur
"at random," in a broad spectrum about the average size. Selection
must impart direction — and be the creative force of evolution —

by differentially preserving those random variants yielding smaller than average phenotypes.

Randomness is a part of Darwinian theory, but it has a very definite and restricted role (lest the central premise of creativity for natural selection be compromised). It operates only in the genesis of raw material — genetic variation. It plays no role at all in the production of evolutionary change — the selective preservation of a portion of this variation to build altered organisms.

Critics of Darwinism, Arthur Koestler for example, have often misunderstood this central tenet of Darwinism. They charge that Darwinism cannot be correct because a world so ordered as ours cannot be built by random processes. But they fail to understand that Darwinism invokes randomness only to generate raw material. It agrees with the critics in arguing that the world's order could only be produced by a conventional deterministic cause — natural selection in this case.

2. *The reductionistic tradition.* The central claim of the synthesis, and the basis for its alleged unifying power, holds that the phenomena of macroevolution, at whatever scale, can be explained in terms of genetic processes that operate within populations. Organisms are the primary Darwinian actors and evolution at all levels is a result of natural selection, working by sorting out individuals within populations (differential reproductive success). This argument reflects a reductionistic tradition, not of course to atoms and molecules of the classic physical version, but rather of such macroevolutionary events as long-term trends to the extended struggle of individual organisms within local populations.

Reduction to struggles among organisms within populations is fundamental to Darwinism and underlies the logic of Darwin's own version of natural selection (Gould, 1982). Darwin developed his theory as a conscious analog to the laissez-faire economics of Adam Smith (Schweber, 1977), which holds as its primary argument that order and harmony within economies does not arise from higher-order laws destined for such effect, but can be justly attained only by letting individuals struggle for personal benefits, thereby allowing order to arise as an unplanned consequence of sorting among competitors. The Darwinism of the modern synthesis is, therefore, a *one-level theory* that identifies struggle among organisms within populations as the causal source of evolutionary change, and views all other styles and descriptions of change as consequences of this primary activity.

3. *The hegemony of adaptation.* If evolutionary change proceeds via the struggle of individuals within populations, then its result must be adaptation. Natural selection operates by the differential reproductive success of individuals better suited to local environments (as a happy result of their combinations of genetic variation). The statistical accumulation of these favored genes within populations must produce adaptation if evolutionary change is controlled by natural selection. Of course, all Darwinians admit that other processes — the random force of genetic drift in particular — can produce evolutionary change as well, but the synthetic theory carefully limits their range and efficacy, so that they play no statistically important role in the net amount of phenotypic change within lineages. Since (under the second argument for extrapolation) long-term trends are nothing but natural selection within populations extended, then the phenomena of macroevolution reduce to natural selection as well and must be similarly adaptive throughout.

II. CURRENT CRITIQUES OF THE CENTRAL LOGIC OF THE SYNTHESIS

All three major premises of the synthetic theory have been criticized in recent years:

1. *Chance as an agent of evolutionary change.* In a major revision of Darwinian logic, chance has been elevated, from its traditional and restricted role as generator of raw material only, to a more active part as agent of evolutionary *change*.

Most debates in natural history center upon issues of relative frequency, not exclusive occurrence. Chance as an agent of evolutionary change in the phenomenon of "genetic drift" has long been recognized as orthodox, but traditional theory so restricted its occurrence and importance that it could play no major role in life's history. The new arguments are distinctive in that they advocate a high relative frequency for chance and make it an important evolutionary agent of change in both the qualitative and quantitative sense. They also award an important role to chance at all levels of the hierarchy of evolutionary causation — at the molecular level of allelic substitution, the domain of speciation, and the largest scope of changing taxonomic composition in mass extinction.

The quasi-clocklike accumulation of DNA differences in phyletic lines, the empirical basis for the so-called "neutral" theory, or "non-Darwinian evolution" (King and Jukes, 1969), only makes sense if selection does not "see" the substitutions and if they, therefore, drift to fixation in a stochastic manner. Most models of sympatric speciation — though the relative frequency of this process remains unresolved and may be quite low — propose a genetic change quick enough to produce reproductive isolation (often by major alterations in number or form of chromosomes) prior to any selective revamping of the new form. The genetic trigger of speciation would therefore be random with respect to the demands of adaptation. I shall have more to say about mass extinction in the next section, but if these debacles really run on a 26-million year cycle (Raup and Sepkoski, 1984) triggered by cometary showers (Alvarez and Muller, 1984), then the reasons for differential survival cannot have much to do with — and must be random with respect to — the deterministic, adaptive struggles of organisms in the preceding normal geological times.

2. *The hierarchical perspective and the nonreducibility of macroevolution.* The material of biology is ordered into a genea-

logical hierarchy of ever more inclusive objects: genes, bodies, demes (local populations of a species), species, and monophyletic clades of species. Although our linguistic habits generally restrict the term "individual" to bodies alone, each unit of this hierarchy maintains the two essential properties that qualify it as an "individual" and therefore (under selectionist theories), as a potential causal agent in its own right — stability in time (with recognizable inception and extinction, and sufficient coherence of form between beginning and end) and ability to replicate with error (a prerequisite for units of selection in Darwin's world). Traditional Darwinian gradualists would deny individuality to species by arguing that they are mere abstractions, names we give to segments of gradually transforming lineages. But under the punctuated equilibrium model (Eldredge and Gould, 1972; Gould and Eldredge, 1977), species are generally stable following their geologically rapid origin, and most evolutionary change occurs in conjunction with events of branching speciation, not by the transformation *in toto* of existing species. Under this model, therefore, species maintain the essential properties of individuals and may be so designated (Eldredge and Cracraft, 1980; Vrba and Eldredge, 1984).

Few evolutionists would deny this hierarchy in a descriptive sense, but traditions of the modern synthesis specify that causality be sought only at the level of organisms — for natural selection operates by sorting organisms within populations. Richard Dawkins has challenged this view, but in the interests of an even further and stricter reductionism (1976, 1982). He argues that genes are the only true causal agents and organisms merely their temporary receptacles. I strongly disagree with Dawkins (Gould, 1983), since I feel that he has confused bookkeeping (which may be done efficiently in terms of genes) with causality. But I feel that he has inadvertently made an important contribution to the theory of causal hierarchy by establishing numerous cases of true gene-level selection — that is, selection upon genes that occurs without a sorting of bodies and that has no effect upon the phenotypes of bodies. The hypothesis of "selfish DNA" as an explanation for iteration of copies in middle-repetitive DNA (with no initial benefit or detriment to organisms at the next hierarchical level) represents the most interesting proposal for independent gene-level selection (Doolittle and Sapienza, 1980; Orgel and Crick, 1980).

If genes can be selected independently of organisms, then we may extend the causal hierarchy upward as well. Deme-level selection has long been advocated by Sewall Wright in his theory of "shifting balance" (Wright, 1931). Species selection may be a more potent force than traditional Darwinian sorting of organisms in both the spread of features within clades and the differential success of some clades over others. True species selection relies upon properties of species as entities — propensity to speciate in particular — that cannot be reduced to characteristics of organisms, and therefore cannot be explained by natural selection operating at its usual level. The expanded hierarchical theory remains Darwinian in spirit — since it advocates a process of selection at several levels of a hierarchy of individuals — but it confutes the central Darwinian logic that evolutionary events at all scales be reduced for causal explanation to the level of organisms within populations (Gould, 1982, 1985).

3. *Critique of adaptation.* A potent critique against the hegemony of adaptation has arisen from the theory of neutralism — the claim that much genetic change accumulates in populations by genetic drift upon allelic variants that are irrelevant to adaptation, and that natural selection therefore cannot recognize. Although these critiques are valid and were historically important in breaking the hegemony of adaptation, I shall bypass them here because I wish to discuss the evolution of phenotypes, and neutral changes, by definition, do not affect phenotypes.

At the level of phenotypes, the critique of adaptation does not claim a discovery of new evolutionary processes that actively produce substantial phenotypic change without natural selection. The

critique remains content with the conventional idea that natural
selection is the only identified agent of substantial and persistent
evolutionary *change*. In what sense, then, can we speak of a
critique of adaptation?

Suppose that every adaptive change brings with it (since organisms are integrated entities) a set of nonadaptive sequelae far
exceeding in number and extent the direct adaptation itself (see
Gould, 1984a and 1984b for specific examples). Suppose then
that these sequelae serve as constraints and channels that power-
fully determine the limits and directions of future evolutionary
change. Natural selection may still be the force that pushes organisms down the channels, but if these channels are the only paths
available, and if they themselves were not constructed as a direct
result of adaptation, then phenotypes are as much determined by
the limits and potentialities set by non-adaptation as by the direct
change produced by natural selection itself.

Of course, traditional Darwinians do not deny that adaptation
entails non-adaptive consequences. This theme is, for example, the
classic material of allometry, a subject named and popularized by
the great Darwinian Julian Huxley (Huxley, 1932; Gould, 1966).
But these consequences are conventionally viewed as superficial,
epiphenomenal and non-constraining; natural selection, after all,
can break an allometric correlation when necessary. Moreover,
although Darwinism does not deny the existence of powerful constraints upon pathways of evolutionary change, the constraints are
attributed to past adaptations for different roles. Thus, features
of the phenotype are either current adaptations or past adaptations
to different circumstances that constrain current change. Adaptation reigns. Darwin himself, a careful student of constraints and
correlations, wrestled long and hard with this problem and finally
resolved it in favor of adaptive supremacy in a key but neglected
passage in the *Origin of Species* (1859, p. 206):

> All organic beings have been formed on two great laws —
> Unity of Type and the Conditions of Existence. By unity of

type is meant that fundamental agreement in structure, which we see in organic beings of the same class, and which is quite independent of their habits of life. . . . The expression of conditions of existence . . . is fully embraced by the principle of natural selection. For natural selection acts by either now adapting the varying parts of each being to its organic and inorganic conditions of life; or by having adapted them during long-past periods of time. . . . Hence, in fact, the law of Conditions of Existence is the higher law; as it includes, through the inheritance of former adaptations, that of Unity of Type.

I believe that our views on the causes of phenotypic change have become stalled in a strict Darwinism that has already offered its valid insights — and that each critique of Darwinism offers an important new perspective. I shall illustrate the potential of each critique to expand our view of evolution in specific cases by discussing their potential impact upon the event of most immediate concern and importance to us — the evolution of human consciousness.

III. Consciousness as Cosmic Accident

Four controlling biases of Western thought — progressivism, determinism, gradualism, and adaptationism — have combined to construct a view of human evolution congenial to our hopes and expectations. Since we evolved late and, by our consciousness, now seem well in control (for better or for worse), the four biases embody a view that we rule by right because evolution moves gradually and predictably toward progress, always working for the best. These four biases have long stood as the greatest impediments to a general understanding and appreciation of the Darwinian vision, with its explicit denial of inherent progress and optimality in the products of evolution.

Yet Darwinism does not confute all our hopes. It still smuggles the idea of progress back into empirical expectation, not by the explicit workings of its basic mechanism (which does, indeed, deny inherent advance), but by an accumulation of superior designs through successive local adaptations (see Gould, 1985, for a resolution of this apparent paradox). All the great modern Darwinians have come to terms with (and supported) the notion of evolutionary progress, even though they recognized that the basic mechanism of natural selection contains no explicit statement about it (Huxley, 1953; Simpson, 1949; Rensch, 1971; Stebbins, 1969; Dobzhansky, 1972). Moreover, in viewing selection as a deterministic process, Darwinism supports our hope that the directions of change have their good reasons. In this Darwinian climate, we may still view the evolution of human consciousness as the predictable end of a long history of increasing mentality. Yet our new ideas about the importance of randomness in evolutionary change — particularly at the highest level of mass extinction — seriously upset this comforting and traditional notion and strongly suggest that we must view the evolution of human consciousness as a lucky accident that occurred only by the fortunate (for us) concatenation of numerous improbabilities. The argument is not based on a waffling theoretical generality, but on a specific empirical claim about a single important event: the Cretaceous mass extinction.

We may summarize the exciting ferment now reorganizing our ideas on mass extinction (see summary in Gould, 1985) by stating that these major punctuations in life's history are more frequent, more sudden, more severe, and more qualitatively different than we had realized before. I believe that Alvarez *et al.* (1980) have now proved their originally startling claim that a large extraterrestrial body struck the earth some 65 million years ago and must, therefore, be viewed as the major trigger of the Cretaceous extinction. Enhanced levels of presumably extraterrestrial iridium (the empirical basis of the Alvarez claim for the Cretaceous) have now been found at other extinction boundaries as well — so we may have the basis for a general theory of mass extinction, not merely a good story for the Cretaceous.

The meaning of the extraterrestrial theory for human conscious-ness as a cosmic accident begins with a basic fact that should be more widely known (but that will surprise most non-professionals, who assume something different) : *dinosaurs and mammals evolved at the same time.* Mammals did not arise later, as superior forms that gradually replaced inferior dinosaurs by competition. Mam-mals existed throughout the 100 million years of dinosaurian domination — and they lived as small, mostly mouse-sized crea-tures in the ecological interstices of a world ruled by large reptiles. They did not get bigger; they did not get better (or at least their changes did nothing to drive dinosaurs toward extinction). They did nothing to dislodge the incumbents; they bided their time.

Structural or mental inferiority did not drive the dinosaurs to extinction. They were doing well, and showing no sign of ceding domination, right until the extraterrestrial debacle unleashed a set of sudden consequences (as yet to be adequately specified, al-though the "nuclear winter" scenario of a cold, dark world has been proposed for the same reasons). Some mammals weathered the storm; no dinosaurs did. We have no reason to believe that mammals prevailed as a result of any feature traditionally asserted to prove their superiority — warm-bloodedness, live bearing, large brains, for example. Their "success" might well be attributed to nothing more than their size — for nothing large and terrestrial got through the Cretaceous debacle, while many small creatures survived.

In any case, had the cometary shower (or whatever) not hit, we have no reason to think that dinosaurs, having dominated the earth for 100 million years, would not have held on for another 65 to continue their hegemony today. In such a case, mammals would probably still be mouse-sized creatures living on the fringes — after all, they had done nothing else for 100 million years before. Moreover, dinosaurs were not evolving toward any form of consciousness. In other words, those comets or asteroids were the *sine quibus non* of our current existence. Without the removal of dinosaurs that they engendered, consciousness would not have evolved on our earth.

IV. EXAPTATION AND THE FLEXIBILITY OF MIND

Strict adaptation entails a paradox for students of evolutionary change. If all structures are well designed for immediate use, where is the flexibility for substantial change in response to severely altered environments? The conventional answer calls upon a phenomenon of "preadaptation" — the idea that structures actively evolved for one use may be fortuitously fitted for easy modification to strikingly different functions (feathers, evolved for thermo-regulation, then available for flight, for example). But preadaptation speaks only of one-for-one substitutions based on previous adaptation. Can we identify a *pool* of flexibility in uncommitted structures?

Vrba and I have argued that strict adaptationism has blinded us to the absence of an important concept in our science of form (Gould and Vrba, 1982). Some evolutionists use "adaptation" for any structure that performs a beneficial function, regardless of its origin. But a long tradition, dating from Darwin himself, restricts "adaptation" to those structures evolved directly by natural selection for their current use. If we accept this stricter definition, what shall we call structures that contribute to fitness but evolved for other reasons and were later coopted for their current role? They have no name at present, and Vrba and I suggest that they be called "exaptations." Preadaptation is, of course, a related concept — a kind of exaptation before the fact (feathers on a running dinosaur are preadaptations for flight; unaltered on a bird, they are exaptations). But preadaptation does not cover the range of exaptation because it refers to structures *adapted* for one role that are fortuitously suited for another. Preadaptation does not cover the large class of structures that never were adaptations for anything, but arose as the numerous non-adaptive sequelae of primary adaptations. These are also available for later cooptation as exaptations (see examples in Gould and Lewontin, 1979, mostly from architecture and anthropology, where the concept does not threaten conventional thought and is therefore easier to grasp and accept). Surely, since non-adaptive sequelae are more numerous than adaptations themselves, the range of exaptive possibility must be set primarily by non-adaptation. Thus, if flexibility is primarily a result of possibilities that remain labile either because they have no current function (potential exaptations) or because their currently adapted structure can do other things just as well (preadaptations), then the major basis of flexibility must lie in non-adaptation. The old adage that flexibility correlates positively with complexity is correct, but the reason is not primarily — as usually stated — that complexity is itself so highly adaptive, but rather that increased complexity implies a vastly greater range of non-adaptive sequelae for any change, and hence a greatly enlarged exaptive pool.

Flexibility and computing power are the interrelated keys to the power of human consciousness. Among the usual reasons cited for extreme flexibility of human consciousness are the biological neoteny that probably keeps our brain in a labile, juvenile state (Gould, 1977) and the unparalleled potential of the non-somatic culture that our brains have made possible. These are indeed the two major reasons for human flexibility, but both are reflections of a single underlying theme: no biological structure has ever been so pregnant with exaptive possibilities as the human brain; no other biological structure has ever produced so many nonadaptive sequelae to its primary adaptation of increased size.

I do not doubt that the brain became large for an adaptive reason (probably a set of complex reasons) and that natural selection brought it to a size that made consciousness possible. But, surely, most of what our brain does today, most of what makes us so distinctively human (and flexible), arises as a consequence of the non-adaptive sequelae, not of the primary adaptation itself — for the sequelae must be so vastly greater in number and possibility. The brain is a complex computer constructed by natural selection to perform a tiny subset of its potential operations. An arm built for one thing can do others (I am now typing with fingers built for other purposes). But a brain built for some functions can do orders of magnitude more simply by virtue of its basic construction as a flexible computer. Never in biological history has evolution built a structure with such an enormous and ramifying set of exaptive possibilities. The basis of human flexibility lies in the unselected capacities of our large brain.

This perspective also suggests that we must radically revise our methodology for thinking about the biological basis of essential human institutions and behaviors. An enormous, and largely speculative, literature attempts to interpret anything important that our brains do today as direct adaptations to the environments that shaped our earlier evolution. Thus, for example, religion may be a modern reflection of behaviors that evolved to cement group coherence among savannah hunters. But religion might as well record our human response to that most terrifying fact that a large brain allowed us to learn (for no directly adaptive reason) — the inevitability of our personal mortality. I suspect that most of our current cognitive life uses the non-adaptive sequelae of a large brain as exaptations, and does not record the direct reasons why natural selection originally fashioned our large brain.

V. Hierarchy and the Simultaneous, Conscious Control of Levels

Hierarchies of inclusion, like the genealogical hierarchy under discussion here, maintain an important property of asymmetry. Sorting at any high level must produce effects at all lower levels by shuffling their units (individuals) as well (see Campbell, 1974, on downward causation). This property of hierarchies is responsible for the causal confusion of reductionists who assume that because lowest-level units—genes in this case—are always sorted, then this sorting (which they confuse with, and call, selection) must record the causal locus of change. But, again, bookkeeping is not causality, and this argument is invalid. Thus, when species selection operates and certain kinds of species are removed from or differentially added to a clade, proportions of organisms and frequencies of genes must also change within the clade—although the cause of sorting resides at the species level.

The converse, however, is not true. Sorting at low levels does not necessarily produce any effect at all upon the character or relative numbers of higher-level individuals. Lower-level sorting may be effectively insulated from any effect upon higher levels. Thus, at least initially, mobile genes may increase their number of copies within genomes without producing any effect upon bodies, demes, or species. This invisibility is the basis of the selfish DNA hypothesis.

Organisms — the quintessential Darwinian actors — normally can only operate directly for themselves. This produces the paradox of overspecialization when benefits to individuals entail eventual extinction of species because bizarre specializations so limit flexibility in the face of environmental change. Imagine what evolutionary possibilities would be opened if this asymmetry could be broken, and if lower-level units could work simultaneously both for their own fitness and for the fitness of those higher units in which they reside. Yet this cannot happen in a world of unconscious objects, for how could a gene work actively for its body, or a body for its species, when individuals only "see" selection at their own level and cannot know (because they are unaffected by) the forces and directions of higher-level selection?

But human consciousness has ruptured this system. We can use conscious thought to break through the bounds of our own level and to understand what we might do as individuals to enhance or injure the groups in which we reside. In short, we can work directly on our own higher-level fitness. We also have the genetic flexibility — since we are not programmed automata — to choose actions injurious to ourselves but beneficial to our groups, even though natural selection has been working only on our individual-level fitness for so long. Thus, we can behave altruistically not only because certain organism-level processes — kin selection and reciprocal altruism — select for self-abnegation as a good Darwinian strategy, but primarily because we can understand the importance of group-level fitness and have the genetic flexibility (probably for non-adaptive reasons, and not necessarily as the result of millennia of kin selection) to act accordingly. In this sense, the strict Darwinian explanations for altruism offered by sociobiology are inadequate.

For the first time in biological history, organisms can actively pursue fitness not only for themselves but at several levels of their own hierarchy. The gain in potential power and flexibility is staggering. We can now speed and alter the evolution of our species at unprecedented rates and effectiveness. We have broken the ordering principles of the evolutionary hierarchy.

This unique mode of evolution also presents new challenges. If we lived in a world of intrinsic harmony, where fitness at one level inevitably enhanced fitness at others, our new abilities would simply allow us to tap a positive feedback loop between individual and species-level fitness *ad majorem hominis generisque gloriam*. But our world is not so pleasant. The components of fitness at one level are just as likely to depress (as in overspecialization) as to enhance fitness at higher levels. Consciousness puts us in the uncomfortable position of being the only species that can directly affect the components of both its individual and species-level fitness — and of finding that they often conflict. What then are we to do? Shall our great athletes press for even higher salaries and imperil the health and finances of their game's organization?

I have argued that three criticisms of strict Darwinism — randomness, non-adaptation, and hierarchy — each has important implications for a revised view of the evolutionary meaning of human consciousness. Some readers might draw a pessimistic message from the coordinated theme that less predictability, less order, less design attended the evolution of our unique mentality. They may be justly reminded of the *Rubaiyat*'s famous couplet,

> Into this Universe, and Why not knowing
> Nor Whence, like Water willy-nilly flowing.

I draw no somber conclusions from these arguments. I do not believe, first of all, that the answer to moral dilemmas about meaning lies with the facts of nature, whatever they may be. Moreover, I see only hope in the flexibility offered to human consciousness by its evolutionary construction. If our mentality evolved for no particular predictable reasons, then we may make of it what we will. If the major activity of our brain records the non-adaptive sequelae of its construction as a powerful computer, then evolutionary adaptation does not specify how we must behave and what we must do. *Vita brevis* to be sure, but what possibilities.

> Ah, make the most of what we yet may spend,
> Before we too into the Dust descend . . .
> Here with a little Bread beneath the Bough . . .
> Oh, Wilderness were Paradise enow!

BIBLIOGRAPHY

ALVAREZ, L., W. ALVAREZ, F. ASARO, AND H. V. MICHEL. 1980. Extraterrestrial cause for the Cretaceous-Tertiary extinction. *Science* 208: 1095–1108.

ALVAREZ, W., AND R. A. MULLER. 1984. Evidence from crater ages for periodic impacts on the Earth. *Nature* 308: 718–20.

CAMPBELL, D. T. 1974. 'Downward Causation' in hierarchically organised biological systems. In F. J. Ayala and T. Dobzhansky, eds., *Studies in the Philosophy of Biology*. London: Macmillan; Berkeley: University of California Press, pp. 179–83.

DARWIN, C. 1859. *On the Origin of Species*. London: J. Murray.

DAWKINS, R. 1976. *The Selfish Gene*. New York: Oxford Univ. Press.

———. 1982. *The Extended Phenotype*. San Francisco: W. H. Freeman.

DOBZHANSKY, T. 1972. The ascent of man. *Social Biology* 19: 367–78.

DOOLITTLE, W. F., AND C. SAPIENZA. 1980. Selfish genes, the phenotype paradigm, and genome evolution. *Nature* 284: 601–3.

ELDREDGE, N., AND S. J. GOULD. 1972. Punctuated equilibria: an alternative to phyletic gradualism. In T. J. M. Schopf, ed., *Models in Paleobiology*. San Francisco: Freeman, Cooper and Co., pp. 82–115.

ELDREDGE, N., AND J. CRACRAFT. 1980. *Phylogenetic Patterns and the Evolutionary Process*. New York: Columbia Univ. Press.

GOULD, S. J. 1966. Allometry and size in ontogeny and phylogeny. *Biol. Rev.* 41: 587–640.

———. 1977. *Ontogeny and Phylogeny*. Cambridge: Harvard Univ. Press.

———. 1982. Darwinism and the expansion of evolutionary theory. *Science* 216: 380–87.

———. 1983. Irrelevance, submission and partnership: the changing role of palaeontology in Darwin's three Centennials, and a modest proposal for macroevolution. In J. Bendall, ed., *Evolution from Molecules to Man*. Cambridge: Cambridge Univ. Press, pp. 347–66.

———. 1984a. Covariance sets and ordered geographic variation in *Cerion* from Aruba, Bonaire and Curacao: A way of studying nonadaptation. *Syst. Zool.* 33 (2): 217–37.

———. 1984b. Morphological channeling by structural constraint: convergence in styles of dwarfing and gigantism in *Cerion*, with a description of two new fossil species and a report on the discovery of the largest *Cerion*. *Paleobiology*.

———. 1985. The paradox of the first tier; an agenda for paleobiology. *Paleobiology*, in press.

GOULD, S. J., AND N. ELDREDGE. 1977. Punctuated equilibria: the tempo and mode of evolution reconsidered. *Paleobiology* 3 (2): 115–51.

GOULD, S. J., AND R. C. LEWONTIN. 1979. The spandrels of San Marco and the Panglossian paradigm: a critique of the adaptationist programme. *Proc. R. Soc. Lond.* B 205: 581–98.

GOULD, S. J., AND ELISABETH S. VRBA. 1982. Exaptation — a missing term in the science of form. *Paleobiology* 8 (1): 4–15.

HUXLEY, J. 1932. *Problems of Relative Growth*. London: MacVeagh.

———. 1942. *Evolution, The Modern Synthesis*. London: Allen and Unwin.

———. 1953. *Evolution in Action*. London: Chatto and Windus.

KING, J. L., AND T. H. JUKES. 1969. Non-Darwinian evolution. *Science* 164: 788.

MAYR, E., AND W. PROVINE. 1980. *The Evolutionary Synthesis.* Cambridge: Harvard Univ. Press.

ORGEL, L. E., AND F. H. C. CRICK. 1980. Selfish DNA: the ultimate parasite. *Nature* 284: 604–7.

RAUP, D. M., AND J. J. SEPKOSKI, JR. 1982. Mass extinctions in the marine fossil record. *Science* 215: 1501–3.

RENSCH, B. 1971. *Biophilosophy.* New York: Columbia Univ. Press.

SCHWEBER, S. S. 1977. The origin of the *Origin* revisited. *J. History Biol.* 10: 229–316.

STEBBINS, G. L. 1969. *The Basis of Progressive Evolution.* Chapel Hill: The University of North Carolina Press.

VRBA, E. S., AND N. ELDREDGE. 1984. Individuals, hierarchies and processes: towards a more complete evolutionary theory. *Paleobiology.*

WRIGHT, S. 1931. Evolution in Mendelian populations. *Genetics.* 16: 97–159.

The Impact of Modern Genetics

DONALD D. BROWN

THE TANNER LECTURES ON HUMAN VALUES

Delivered at
Brasenose College, Oxford University

May 15 and 16, 1984

DONALD D. BROWN was born in Cincinnati, Ohio, in 1931, and educated at Dartmouth College and the University of Chicago, where he received an M.D. degree. After an internship in New Orleans, he served two years as a commissioned officer in the U.S. Public Health Service at the National Institutes of Health, doing full-time research. He went to the Pasteur Institute in Paris for a year before joining the Department of Embryology of the Carnegie Institution of Washington, where he began as a postdoctoral fellow, became a Staff Member in 1962 and Director in 1976. Dr. Brown is now a Professor in the Department of Biology of the Johns Hopkins University. He has received several awards and honorary degrees and has been honored by election to the National Academy of Science, the American Academy of Arts and Sciences, and the American Philosophical Society. He has written about one hundred scientific papers.

I. GENETIC ENGINEERING: ITS PROMISE AND PROBLEMS

The discovery of the double helical structure of DNA in 1953 has played a role in modern genetics analogous to the impact that the discovery of the atom had for nuclear physics during the first half of this century. Prior to 1953, genes were defined as elements that obeyed the well-known Mendelian rules of heredity. A defective gene was often recognized by a change in some visible trait. Among the earliest known examples of genes that obey Mendel's laws are those whose mutations cause certain diseases such as hemophilia and sickle cell anemia. It has been known for a long time that the occurrence of these diseases in affected families is predictable. The advent of genetic chemistry made us consider for the first time how the DNA molecule could encode such complex traits. Discoveries since 1953 have taught us how to work with the genetic material as a chemical reagent. We have learned about the structure of DNA and its chemistry. This information explains well-known biological functions of genes such as their ability to reproduce themselves exactly and how information is encoded and expressed by genes.

It is not possible to talk reasonably about the impact of these discoveries without understanding something about the science of genetic biochemistry. I propose to explain it as briefly as possible before evaluating the risks and benefits of genetic engineering.

Genetic biochemistry

DNA has two important functions that it must carry out in living cells. It duplicates itself, and it encodes protein. Inherent in the structure of DNA are explanations for both functions.

[77]

DNA consists of four building blocks called nucleotides or "bases," designated by the letters A, G, C, and T, that are linked together to form very long molecules. Two of these long chains are intertwined to form a double helix. The key rule used by Watson and Crick to account for how the two strands are held together is called base complementarity.[1] Wherever there is an A in one strand there must be a T opposite it in the second strand. Likewise, G residues face C's. A is complementary to T, and G is complementary to C. Thus, the exact order of bases in one strand precisely specifies the order of bases in the other by the rules of base complementarity. This is a way to form two identical DNA molecules where only one had existed previously. Not only does this explain self-duplication, but the phenomenon of base complementarity is at the heart of genetic engineering and biotechnology. All methods used to find genes and manipulate them depend upon base complementarity.

Proteins are polymers consisting of twenty building blocks called amino acids linked together. The linear order of the DNA bases in a gene specifies the exact linear order of amino acids in proteins. It is a very simple code in which each arrangement of three bases is translated into only one amino acid. DNA also contains signals for the control of gene expression. The expression of a gene leads ultimately to the synthesis of the protein that it encodes. In a skin cell, the genes for skin proteins (keratin) are actively expressed, but the genes for blood proteins (globin) are silent. This differential gene expression is influenced by signals in DNA near and within genes. The understanding of how genes work in cells is one of the most exciting and fundamental unsolved problems of biology. I will use it as an example in the second lecture to show how modern methods are resolving important biological questions.

---

[1] J. D. Watson and F. H. C. Crick. A Structure for deoxyribose nucleic acids. *Nature* 171 (1953): 737–38.

This is a great oversimplification of the majesty of DNA and genetic biochemistry, but it contains the salient facts to help us understand what genetic engineering is likely to be used for. To summarize:

DNA is a template for its own duplication.

DNA encodes proteins and the code is universal in all organisms studied to date from bacteria and viruses to man.

DNA has signals for the control of its expression, but these signals are not universal.

Advances in genetic biochemistry since the discovery of DNA structure in 1953 have elucidated how living cells carry out these processes. It is these details and the methods devised to study them that have made genetic engineering possible. The revolution in genetic biochemistry following that first great theoretical discovery has been marked by practicality, not theory; the development of new methods plays the greatest role in answering what are really very old questions.

Working with genes

It has been a surprise to scientists that modern methods have made DNA the easiest of all biological macromolecules to study and manipulate. It was not so long ago that DNA was a sticky mess and just about intractable for analysis. Now there are many methods available for isolating a gene of interest by recombinant DNA techniques.[2] Reagents cleave DNA at specified bases, ligate pieces of DNA together regardless of their origin, replicate DNA, and make precise mutations in genes that can then be perpetuated by recombinant DNA methods. The exact order of bases in long stretches of DNA can be determined with ease. The sequence of bases of the entire genome of the simplest viruses has been determined. In the old days, we would discover a new protein and

[2] S. N. Cohen. The manipulation of genes. *Sci. Am.* 233 (1975): 24–33.

then know that there must be a gene for it. Nowadays, we sequence DNA, enter it into a computer, and are told that it encodes a protein and the exact amino acid sequence of that protein. If the protein, or one that resembles it, has been discovered already by someone else, the computer will tell us so. Another very important advance for genetic engineering is transformation, in which pure genes are introduced into living cells or organisms in such a way that they function.[3]

Genes encode proteins. Insulin is a protein, but penicillin is not. Penicillin does not have a gene; it is made step by step in mold cells by a group of protein catalysts called enzymes. Therefore, it would take many genes to instruct a living organism to make penicillin, but only one gene for insulin. Consider also genetic diseases. Hemophilia, sickle cell anemia, and cystic fibrosis are examples of simple genetic diseases. They obey Mendel's rules of inheritance since each is caused by a defect in a single gene. In the case of hemophilia, it is the gene for a protein involved in blood clotting. Sickle cell anemia is the result of a mutation wherein one of the 438 bases encoding the blood protein globin has been changed, resulting in a replacement of one of the 146 amino acids of globin; the altered protein cannot bind oxygen as well as the normal globin, which causes severe consequences for the patient. The basic defect of cystic fibrosis is not known, but it can be predicted confidently that the gene encoding some essential but, as yet, unidentified protein is mutated.

Contrast these diseases with diabetes and certain kinds of heart disease. If your parents have either of these diseases, then you will have an increased chance to have them as well. These are complex genetic diseases with more than one gene involved, so they are not inherited in a simple manner.

---

[3] A. Pellicer, M. Wigler, R. Axel, and S. Silverstein. The transfer and stable integration of the HSV thymidine kinase gene into mouse cells. *Cell* 14 (1978): 133–41.

These simple precepts can help us to distinguish what genetic engineering can do with reasonable certainty soon or in the future from what it is unlikely ever to be able to perform. Proteins can be made by genetic engineering — certain hormones, vaccines, clotting factors, perhaps silk and wool. Defects in specific proteins caused by simple genetic mutations might be treated by gene replacement therapy with the gene for that protein. The cure of diseases or alteration of traits that are the result of the interactions of many genes will not be candidates for simple genetic engineering as we know it today. Organ transplantation would seem to be more promising. These concepts are important for an understanding of what biotechnology can do, and they are also the basis for a rational discussion of the hazards of these methods. I now wish to enumerate some kinds of genetic engineering starting with schemes already in practice, progressing toward those more in the realm of science fiction.

The microorganism as a factory

There has been a worldwide shortage of the protein insulin, which traditionally has been purified from the pancreases of cows and pigs. These animal forms of insulin also differ from human insulin in two amino acid residues. This seemingly small difference occasionally results in an adverse reaction in diabetics who receive the insulin. Their systems reject bovine insulin as a foreign protein by making antibodies against it. Eli Lilly now markets human insulin that is synthesized by microorganisms genetically engineered to contain the gene for human insulin. This is the first practical commercial application of genetic engineering in which microorganisms (bacteria or yeast) are used as living factories for making large amounts of one particular protein (or gene) in great purity.

The steps required to engineer a bacteria with the gene for insulin have become routine in research laboratories. The major technical feat was to detect the insulin gene in the presence of the thousands of other genes in a mixture of crude human DNA. The insulin gene is present in human DNA in about one part per million. The basis for this crucial assay is the base complementarity mentioned earlier. The order of bases in the insulin gene are exact and not found in any other gene. If one has a piece of DNA (called a probe) in which the order of bases is complementary to part of the insulin gene, the probe can be made to bind specifically to the insulin gene. The first step in isolating a gene is usually to break the crude DNA into smaller fragments and splice each fragment to a piece of bacterial or viral DNA (called the vector). These recombinant molecules are then introduced one per bacterium. A population of bacteria containing the entire DNA content of another species is referred to as a library. One needs only to sort through the library with the probe to find bacteria containing the gene of interest.

The bacterium containing the insulin gene will breed true, replicating the foreign gene along with the vector and its own chromosome. The insulin gene will not make insulin in the bacteria because the signals needed for its correct expression in a human are different from those in the bacterium; more genetic engineering is needed. Bacterial DNA containing signals recognized by bacteria are spliced to the insulin gene. Now the metabolic machinery of the bacteria recognizes the gene and insulin is made.

Mutations used to be introduced laboriously into a gene by mutagenizing organisms and then selecting among survivors for mutations in that particular gene. Now the gene is purified, a base change or a deletion is placed at any location desired, and then the altered gene is cloned in a bacterium.[4]

Another example of this sort of genetic engineering has been its application to a group of animal proteins called interferon.

[4] M. Smith and S. Gillam, "Constructed mutants using synthetic oligodeoxyribonucleotides as site-specific mutagens," in J. K. Setlow and A. Hollaender, eds., *Genetic Engineering*, vol. 3 (New York: Plenum Press, 1981), pp. 1–32.

These proteins have antiviral and perhaps antitumor activity — enough promise at any rate to make their production the goal of a number of biotechnology companies. Interferons are produced by cells in the tiniest amounts. The extraction of living tissues resulted over the years in the partial purification of a small amount of interferon. There was just enough material to tantalize scientists by its biological activity, but never enough to prove conclusively the value of interferons for treatment of any disease. However, now genes for many kinds of interferons have been isolated, fitted with appropriate signals to insure their expression, and grown in bacteria and yeast. Unlimited amounts of pure interferons are now available for testing. One liter of bacteria containing a gene for interferon properly engineered for expression produces far more interferon in an hour than all of the interferon ever extracted from animal tissues and cultured cells. The engineered interferon is pure — the tissue-extracted protein is impure. In addition, variants of interferon are easily made by mutating the gene and then screening the product for activity. This would have been impossible before recombinant DNA technology.

Behind the commercial applications is an extraordinary number of basic research experiments in which bacteria have been used to isolate genes from every imaginable source, plant and animal. Thanks to this recombinant DNA methodology we have learned a great deal about the structure and function of genes especially in higher organisms. Previous notions of gene structure, function, and evolution have been revised drastically because of these powerful methods.

Hazards of the microorganism as a factory

The first hazards of genetic engineering that were addressed were those stemming from the kinds of experiments I have just described. What is the likelihood that a perfectly well-meaning scientist might introduce a gene into a bacterium that would alter the organism drastically with unpredictable results. Would the bacteria now grow in new ecological niches or produce some dangerous product that was not suspected? The uncertainty about such an incident led scientists to police themselves and set forth guidelines for their own research in 1976. These rules were institutionalized in a number of countries and exist today in the United States in modified form.[5]

Even the most ardent critics of this work in 1976, when the debates began, now agree that potential laboratory accidents do not constitute a danger to the public. This conclusion comes from many kinds of evidence. The microorganisms used for gene cloning do not grow outside of the laboratory — and especially not in the intestinal tract of man. Pathogenicity is a highly evolved and rather fragile state. Very few microorganisms out of the enormous variety that exist in nature are pathogenic to man. These organisms are finicky in their growth requirements because of their specialized natures. A bacterium is a finely tuned organism dependent on the integrated functions of about 5,000 genes. The introduction of one foreign gene will not drastically change its general behavior. Complex traits such as the ability to grow in a new environment (the human gut, for example) are themselves the result of many genes with integrated, highly evolved functions. An analogy would be the introduction of one extra transistor at random into an AM radio that already has 5,000 of them carefully and precisely connected. Either nothing at all would happen, or the radio would work less well. The AM radio would not turn into an FM radio.

The microorganism that is disseminated

After eight years of considering hazards posed by microorganisms used as a factory, we have now reached the next level of

[5] The Recombinant DNA Advisory Committee (RAC) supervises and approves all recombinant DNA research that is funded by the National Institutes of Health of the United States. Other agencies have chosen to abide by the RAC's oversight.

concern — the purposeful dissemination of a genetically engineered microorganism to do the work previously reserved for chemicals. An example that is being debated in the U.S. now has to do with a serious agricultural problem in California. A bacterium that colonizes certain crop plants nucleates ice crystal formation that kills the plant. Scientists have isolated a mutated strain of the bacteria which has lost this trait but, as nearly as they can tell, is identical to the parent strain in every other way. They want to field test the mutant strain by spraying it on plants in the hope that it will replace the deleterious strain. The NIH Recombinant DNA Advisory Committee have examined all of the data and concluded that it is safe to proceed. Dissidents have taken the matter to court.

Genetically engineered microorganisms are going to be used for many purposes previously reserved for chemicals. A bacterium that digests oil has been patented but not yet used or approved for use. This is a good example to help put the pros and cons of dissemination into perspective. Oil spills are now contained by pouring detergents on the oil and then trying to vacuum up the mixture. It is not terribly efficient, nor do we understand damage that may be caused by the detergent, but at least the amount of detergent added is under control. Bacteria can proliferate, and therein lies the fear. A skeptic will say that the bacteria may digest the oil spill, but what is to keep them from continuing to grow and spread? Will they infect the gastanks of our cars? There are, however, several advantages of using an engineered microorganism to do a job previously done by a detergent or a pesticide. The very methods that produce a useful bacterium can help to make it safe. Genetic engineering can introduce traits that enfeeble a bacterium so that it will self-destruct. An example in the case of the oil-eating bacterium might be mutations in life-sustaining genes that make the bacteria sensitive to high temperatures. The bacteria are sprayed over the oil and digest it until the ambient temperature rises above a certain level. Then they all die. Bacteria are biodegradable.

Each application of biotechnology must be scrutinized in every bit as much detail as new drugs and new chemicals before they are disseminated. Existing or new agencies must assume these responsibilities.

Genetic engineering of plants

In my opinion, some of the greatest societal benefits of genetic engineering will come from applications to agricultural problems. Improvement of plants has always been a highly empirical procedure. Individual plants are selected for traditional breeding because they show a bit more of some desired trait — for example size, ability to grow in poor soil, or pest resistance. Thus, a crop plant is gradually improved over a period of many years. Many of these traits are obviously the result of many genes working in an integrated fashion and thus more difficult to isolate, clone, study, and then transfer from one plant to another. However, other characteristics seem especially suited for improvement by modern genetics. An example would be the quality of some particular protein in a popular food crop. The major protein of corn, for example, is low in the amino acid lysine, an essential amino acid for humans. If the gene for that protein could be altered so that the protein contained more lysine, corn would be a more nutritional foodstuff. Plant genetics requires the patience to breed and select individual plants with very long life cycles. However, some plant cells can now be cultured *in vitro*, genetically transformed, and then grown into whole plants.

I am unaware of any new hazards posed by applications of modern plant genetics that require different supervision from what already exists.

Genetic engineering of animals

Selective breeding, freezing of sperm and embryos, artificial insemination, and surrogate motherhood are done commercially and/or experimentally with mammals. Individual genes have been introduced into the fertilized eggs of mice and integrated permanently into their genome. These transferred genes can function as exemplified by the introduction of a gene for growth hormone into a mouse embryo, resulting in an abnormally large mouse.[6] From the standpoint of basic research, the most exciting advance in the past few years has been the genetic transformation of fruit flies (*Drosophila*).[7] Many of the rules of animal genetics were derived over the years from studies with fruit flies because of the species' simplicity and short life cycle. Genes are injected into fertilized eggs near the region that will form future germ cells, and the genes are incorporated into egg or sperm as the cells develop. The distinction between germ cell and somatic cell transformation is the source of major controversy, and we will discuss the matter shortly. However, when used as an adjunct method for fruit fly genetics, genetic transformation provides a remarkable opportunity to study gene structure and function. Transformation of genes injected into germ cells of mice also occurs, so we can conclude that the tools are certainly at hand for introducing foreign genes into both germ cells and somatic cells of humans.

What is already done with humans

Before arguing what should or shouldn't be done with humans, it is worth summarizing what already happens either naturally or by intervention.

---

[6] R. D. Palmiter, R. L. Brinster, R. E. Hammer, M. E. Trumbauer, M. G. Rosenfeld, N. C. Birnberg, and R. M. Evans. Dramatic growth of mice that develop from eggs microinjected with metallothionein-growth hormone fusion gene. *Nature* 300 (1982): 611–15.

[7] A. C. Spradling and G. M. Rubin. Transposition of cloned P elements into *Drosophila* germ line chromosomes. *Science* 218 (1982): 341–47; G. M. Rubin and A. C. Spradling. Genetic transformation of *Drosophila* with transposable element vectors. *Science* 218 (1982): 348–53.

A few percent of all humans are members of clones. Of course, these are identical twins. The definition of cloning is the vegetative production of two cells (or individuals) from one cell (or individual) without sexual mating. The billions of cells in our bodies are cloned from the original fertilized egg. Identical twins occur when a fertilized egg cleaves, and the daughter cells separate to form two individuals.

Artificial insemination of fertile females using donor sperm has been an accepted procedure for a long time, when the husband is infertile. Recently, surrogate mothers have been employed by infertile couples. This arrangement seems to generate opposition more because of possible financial impropriety than for ethical reasons. *In vitro* fertilization is a relatively recent way to help some infertile couples produce children from their own egg and sperm.

An increasing number of genetic diseases and abnormalities can be diagnosed *in utero* with the option to terminate pregnancies, a decision that causes more controversy than almost anything else that occurs in medicine.

I mention these diverse natural or human interventions because they are all relevant to one or more points of controversy about genetic engineering that face us today.

Abortion

Modern biology is increasing the number of genetic conditions that can be diagnosed *in utero*. In some cases, accurate prenatal diagnosis may decrease the use of abortion where previously the threat of an abnormality was not considered worth the risk. Even the most ardent believer in free choice (as I am) realizes that the dilemma of the genetic counselor is increasing. For example, Huntington's chorea is a disease caused by a simple dominant mutation whose symptoms do not begin until middle age but can then be guaranteed to progress miserably to the victim's death.

Recent experiments show that DNA technology can diagnose potential victims *in utero* about forty years before they will display the symptoms.[8]

It is generally feared that selective abortion might be used some day on a very large scale in societies where female children are considered a liability. In my opinion, there is real potential here for misuse. Perhaps this has not been discussed as much as other matters because the methods for sex selection of embryos have been available for a long time but not abused, at least on a significant scale. Some genetic counselors refuse to divulge the sex of embryos after routine amniocentesis.

I cannot resist addressing one other issue in the abortion debate. When does life begin? This question obsesses bioethicists, theologians, and legislators. Does life begin with a living cell? The onset of brain waves? The time when a fetus can live outside the mother? Or even when a child can live without parental protection? It is not a scientific question but rather a social, political, religious, or cultural one. Even practical considerations will outweigh scientific ones. Laws must be made to protect individuals, but the decision as to when this protection should begin will be agonized over by each society with little help from scientists. The fact that scientific progress has enabled babies to survive an increasingly premature delivery will not change this basic social dilemma.

Gene therapy

We are learning more about the genetic basis of disease. For simple genetic diseases the exact gene that is defective can be determined. Precise gene therapy would be the replacement of a defective gene with a normal one. This can be done today in only one organism, yeast.[9] Many of the steps that are needed for gene

[8] J. F. Gusella et al. A polymorphic DNA marker genetically linked to Huntington's disease. *Nature* 306 (1983): 234–38.

[9] K. Struhl. The new yeast genetics. *Nature* 305 (1983): 391–97.

therapy have been established already in organisms other than man; in a few years they will be applicable to humans.

Correction of a defective gene in somatic cells might be done by culturing a piece of a patient's tissue, introducing the normal gene properly engineered with the correct signals for expression into the cells in culture, selecting those cells transformed with the normal gene, growing large amounts of this transformed tissue, and then reintroducing this tissue into the patient. Most bioethicists concerned with human genetic manipulations do not seem concerned with this scheme because it would affect only individual patients. But is that the case? Here is an individual who might have died at an early age from a genetic disease but who will now be a functionally normal person with mutant germ cells capable of breeding and disseminating the defective gene to his/her progeny. Whereas, if a defect could be corrected in egg and sperm cells as well as somatic cells, the children would benefit as well as the afflicted parent.

The issue of inviolability of germ cells in humans is a vague one which is defended more from gut instincts than from genuine reason. We decided long ago to intercede on behalf of the ill and the weak. Evolution of most living things has come under the capricious influence of man. Will simple gene therapy lead to parents (or governments) controlling the physical and intellectual traits of children? This is the concern that we hear. But each complex trait is the product of many genes, so even the ability to do this is not on the horizon. Is it even a future concern? Questions of genetic manipulation of man and all other controversies raised by genetic engineering and science must be viewed in perspective.

Perspective

A favorite example of perspective goes something like this. Hundreds of thousands of Americans die each year directly or indirectly due to cigarette smoking; there are about 50,000 deaths from automobile accidents each year. Perhaps there are one or two deaths from shark attacks world wide. On a crowded day at a southern California beach if someone yells "Shark," thousands will clear out of the water, jump into their cars, and light cigarettes.

There have been perhaps several hundred instances of *in vitro* fertilization, yet there are hundreds of thousands of infertile couples who want babies.

There is more concern about the rights of embryos than about the millions of children who starve around the world, a problem exacerbated by burgeoning populations often out of control.

At a recent meeting to discuss the advances in life sciences and the concerns that they raised, I heard the following abuse of perspective. A bioethicist predicted the impact of modern research for good and evil. On the one hand he thought it likely that modern genetics would contribute to curing diseases and to the elimination of hunger and poverty, but the price would be what he called "dehumanization." The analogy was not with Orwell but with Huxley's "Brave New World." We would be disease free, well-fed zombies enjoying the "feelies." I suspect that this man had never been really sick or poor, because *these* are conditions that are really dehumanizing. One hears this kind of vague and abstract criticism of modern genetics. It simply does not provide a useful starting point for debate, except in one respect: There is guaranteed to be some risk associated with each benefit.

The military problem

In 1969, the United States unilaterally renounced biological warfare and destroyed all its stores. In 1972, at the Biological Weapon Convention more than one hundred countries signed an international agreement outlawing all biological and toxin weapons. Recently, there have been accusations that Russia has used mycotoxins in its struggle to subdue Afghanistan and in the so-called "yellow-rain" reported in Southeast Asia. In a series of articles in the *Wall Street Journal* during April of 1984, a writer, whose sources seem mainly to be unnamed Russian expatriates, claims that the Soviets are trying to perfect new biological weapons using modern genetic methods.[10] These are very provocative accusations in an atmosphere of international distrust. Such sensational studies can have very mischievous results. There is no undisputed example of the use of biological warfare since the Convention. The reported incidents mentioned above are highly controversial, and in the opinion of some of the most objective accounts the accusations are without merit.

It should be noted that it would be hard to construct a virus more deadly than some of the ones that occur naturally, or to make in the laboratory a toxin more dangerous than some well-known examples.

Dealing with the risks and benefits of biology

Many of the benefits of modern biology are easy to assess. They include the detection and cure of many diseases. For the first time, in my opinion, we have real insight into the cause of cancer. There are normal genes that can cause cancer when they mutate. We don't know yet how these genes work, but techniques of modern genetics which led to the discovery of these genes in the first place will provide these insights. In the next ten years we are going to understand better and perhaps even cure some of the most serious diseases that afflict mankind, such as diabetes, arteriosclerosis, parasitic diseases, the common cold, cystic fibrosis, certain kinds of arthritis, immune diseases, and infectious diseases, just to name a few. A molecular basis for at least some kinds of schizophrenia will be found. We will learn about the biochemistry of the ageing process, which also has a strong genetic com-

10 W. Kucewicz in *The Wall Street Journal*, April 23, 25 and 27, 1984.

ponent. This doesn't guarantee prolongation of life, but rather an improvement of the quality of life in old age. We need sensitive assays for the effects of chemicals, pollutants, and drugs as causative agents of birth defects like those developed to determine carcinogenic potential. There have yet to be developed simple, safe, and reversible contraceptives for males.

I have already mentioned the influence that modern genetics will have on agriculture and the use of biology to meet needs previously served by chemicals. This could have a salutary effect on the environment. Indeed, modern genetics is expected to help clean up the environment.

Every powerful new technology brings potential for misuse. Biotechnology is often compared with nuclear physics, which brought us the Bomb. Perhaps a fairer comparison is with the computer or electronics industries. These are both nonpolluting industries with many applications, yet we can list misuses of these technologies.

So it will be with biotechnology. If a new drug or chemical is produced by these methods it must be tested for safety with rigor and intelligence. Genetic manipulations on humans can proceed if testing for safety is thorough and objective, and if all experimentation and applications require the strictest control and especially the informed consent of human subjects. There are existing rules and agencies, boards, and committees that are empowered to protect the public against new products and individuals against capricious experimentation by scientists.

If we are to have the benefits with minimal risks, we must prepare to review each problem as it arises. There is no simple solution. Much rests with the quality of our governmental institutions. Enforcement of individual rights and safety has always been their responsibility. They must be kept current with the progress of biotechnology by informed scientists. Science is as sensitive to interference as any art form, so its regulation is a delicate matter. A fine balance needs to be struck between regulation of science and nourishment of the scientific enterprise. One need only glance at the magnitude of society's unsolved problems that this technology might help to solve to conclude that we must take the risk.

II. HOW NEW METHODS IN BIOLOGY ARE SOLVING OLD PROBLEMS

From information stored in eggs and sperm, a developmental timetable is established that precisely determines the formation of about one- to two hundred different cell types in an adult organism. The timing of gene expression must be flawless, otherwise a birth defect will ensue. About 5 percent of all live human births have some sort of congenital anomaly. Half of these malformations are genetic in origin.

Embryogenesis is so complex that most researchers study some tiny aspect, preferably a simple contained system, with the hope that answers can be generalized. In the first lecture, I mentioned how modern methods are playing a role in our understanding of gene control in development. I will summarize here some of the varied ways by which living cells control the expression of their genes during development.[11] It is an area of current research so active that this list will be incomplete; new mechanisms are being uncovered weekly.

In order to put this problem in perspective, I begin with a brief and rather biased history of the field of embryology or developmental biology, as it is now called. At the beginning of this century embryology flourished closely coupled with genetics. The great early embryologists, such as Boveri and Morgan, were geneticists. In the 1920s "experimental embryology" was the popular way to study the field. This approach used animals like chickens and frogs that are not suited for classical genetics. Experimental

---

[11] D. D. Brown. Gene expression in eukaryotes. *Science* 211 (1981): 667–74.

embryology mapped the fate of cells and tissues and their changing capacity to develop. Surgical manipulations transplanted pieces of embryonic material. This led to ideas about how cells moved during embryogenesis and how one tissue could instruct another one ("embryonic induction"). Despite the importance of concepts raised during the thirties and forties, experimental embryology had, in one sense, a detrimental effect on the field because it split embryology from the burgeoning fields of genetics and biochemistry. Experimental embryologists considered themselves members of a special discipline when, in fact, they were studying a set of questions. They needed the concepts and methods that could be provided by other areas of biology. For fifty years genetics and embryology were separate.

Another feature which emerged in those days of experimental embryology was the overwhelming complexity of embryogenesis. It had a stultifying effect on the field. Young scientists were frightened off, and embryologists seemed to be proud of the impenetrability of their subject. They advanced the notion that answers would only come from studying an entire organism, the whole being greater than the sum of its parts.

Biochemical embryology followed experimental embryology. Biochemists homogenized embryos and measured the changes in various molecules with developmental stages. They confirmed what anyone could deduce, namely, changes occurred not only in visible structures but in molecules as well. There was little intellectual communication between "biochemical embryologists" of the forties and fifties and the authors of the truly innovative advances in biochemistry that were occurring at the same time. Biochemical embryologists studied chickens, frogs, and sea urchins; geneticists studied fruit flies (*Drosophila*) and to some extent the mouse. There were no known mutants in chickens, frogs, and sea urchins, and no biochemistry carried out with fruit flies. In fact, up until five or ten years ago, there was not a single mutant identified in *Drosophila* that encoded a specific protein.

Most mutants invariably caused some morphological defect. Nowadays, there are many genes encoding proteins in fruit flies that have been identified and characterized, but this is the result of modern genetic biochemistry.

Immunologists studied rabbits, went to their own meetings, and spoke a language all their own. Immunology was a self-contained discipline. The effect of having scientists outside the field apply modern molecular methods to immunology is instructive for a student of science history. In the past ten years the most fundamental problems of immunology have been solved by outsiders applying new methods previously alien to the field.

Plant biology is another example of the segregation of science. Many universities still have separate departments for plant and animal biology. The American Society of Developmental Biology attempts to integrate botany and zoology by alternating its presidency each year between plant and animal scientists. However, modern methods are accomplishing a less artificial integration as techniques learned from studying one kind of organism can now be applied to all.

New and powerful methods are bringing biologists together. We can now perform genetics at will on frogs and chickens, biochemistry on fruit flies and mice, and both genetics and biochemistry on plants.

The summary of known developmental control mechanisms that follows will give some idea of how organisms control the expression of their genes. I divide these two into categories — gene alteration and gene activation. In the former, the genes are literally changed, that is, lost, amplified, or rearranged. By the later, I mean that the genes are unaltered, but their expression is controlled.

Gene alteration

The earliest known example of gene alteration is called chromosome diminution. In 1903, the great embryologist and geneti-

cist Theodore Boveri showed that the parasitic worm *Ascaris* loses
genetic material from most of its cells during early cleavage stages
of the embryo.[12] This also occurs in some, but not all, crustaceans,
insects, and worms. It is clearly not a general phenomenon of all
embryos. The only cells in *Ascaris* embryos that do not lose genes
are those that give rise to the sperm and egg (germ) cells of the
adult. All of the body (somatic) cells are affected. Most embryos
actually set aside their future germ cells in early development even
though they do not undergo chromosome diminution of somatic
cells. The germ cells do not divide during embryogenesis when
the animal's tissues are forming. Only when this process is com-
pleted will the germ cells then find their place in the embryo and
divide to form a functional gonad.

Some years ago, Igor Dawid and I[13] and, independently, Joseph
Gall[14] at Yale discovered another mechanism of gene alteration
which we called "gene amplification." In this case, a specific gene
is actually duplicated. The example that we studied occurs in the
growing egg cell (oocyte) of frogs, fish, and many (but not all)
other animals. Oocytes grow to enormous size and synthesize certain cytoplasmic constituents in huge amounts. One of these is an
essential component for protein synthesis called the ribosome. The
oocyte, which is a single cell, can synthesize as many ribosomes
in a unit of time as many thousands of the most active body cells
of a frog. Each ribosome consists of three RNA molecules and
about one hundred different proteins. More than one genetic
mechanism enables an oocyte to make such a huge amount of
ribosomes. Two of the RNA molecules are encoded for by genes
that are amplified more than one thousand-fold early in the
growth of the oocyte. This gene amplification is a mechanism by

[12] T. Boveri. Die Entwicklung von *Ascaris megalocephala* mit besonderer
Rucksicht auf die Kernverhaltnisse: Festschr. f. C. von Kupffer XIII (1899).

[13] D. D. Brown and I. B. Dawid. Specific gene amplification in oocytes. *Science*
160 (1968): 272–80.

[14] J. G. Gall. Differential synthesis of the genes for ribosomal RNA during
amphibian oogenesis. *Proc. Nat. Acad. Sci. U.S.A.* 60 (1968): 553–60.

which the cell produces more of a given product. It makes more
genes first and with these extra genes it can then synthesize more
RNA. There is, however, a third RNA molecule in each ribosome
called 5S ribosomal RNA, which we have also studied. There is
an auxiliary set of genes for 5S RNA that are present in the
chromosomes of all cells of the frog, but these genes are only
expressed in the oocyte where the demand for 5S RNA is so
great.[15] In all other cells, the "oocyte"-specific genes are present,
but they are silent.

Recently, gene amplification has been extended to other systems. There are now instances of genes other than those for ribosomes that have been shown to be amplified as part of the developmental program. A related phenomenon, which I refer to as
"forced gene amplification" has medical implications.[16] When a
cell (animal or bacterial) is challenged with a drug that can kill
it, the cell can escape the effects of the drug if it can metabolize
the drug. Often this metabolic machinery exists in a cell, but not
in large enough amounts to cope with high doses of the drug.
Resistant cells can emerge. For example, tumors will be suppressed for a time by chemotherapy, but resistant cells will often
grow. A cell learns to overcome the drug by increasing the amount
of its metabolic machinery through making more genes for that
machinery. Another important example of gene amplification
occurs in some cancerous cells in which gene amplification has
occurred. Apparently too much of certain gene products will lead
to cancerous changes.

About forty years ago, Barbara McClintock, studying at the
Carnegie Institution's Department of Genetics in Cold Spring
Harbor, New York, discovered transposable genetic elements in

[15] D. D. Brown. How a simple animal gene works. *The Harvey Lectures* 76 (1982): 27–44.

[16] R. T. Schimke, F. W. Alt, R. E. Kellems, R. J. Kaufman, and J. R. Bertino. Amplification of folate reductase genes in methotrexate-resistant cultured mouse cells. *Cold Spring Harbor Symp. Quant. Biol.* 42 (1977): 649–58.

maize (corn).[17] She noted that certain kinds of genetic mutations were unstable and the very characteristic of instability itself was genetically inherited. Through cytogenetics and the breeding of mutant plants, she concluded that the instability was due to genes that were able to move around the chromosomes, entering and leaving other stationary genes. When a transposable element moved into another gene, the activity of the stationary gene was often abolished. When the element moved out again, the gene could once again function normally. This is one of the great stories of unrewarded and unrecognized science. In retrospect, however, it is not surprising that scientists could not understand the significance of these bizarre findings. (It was fortunate that she worked at a research institution where applying for grants was not required.) The ramifications of transposable elements grow daily, as well as the realization of their importance. I will give some examples of genetic rearrangement.

The movement of genes from one part of the genome to another can be divided into those events not programmed into the developmental timetable and those that are an integral part of the life cycle of an organism. The best-known example of the latter type is the immune system.[18] In sperm and eggs, the functional genes for antibodies are not found next to each other. During the development of the cells that make antibodies, the genes for antibodies become rearranged so that they can then function. If gene amplification is the cell's way of making large amounts of a few kinds of molecules, then genetic rearrangement is a way that a population of cells can make many closely related molecules. Gene amplification fulfills a need for quantity, while rearrangement provides diversity of gene expression.

[17] B. McClintock. Controlling elements and the gene. *Cold Spring Harbor Symp. Quant. Biol.* 21 (1956): 197–216.

[18] S. Tonegawa, C. Brack, N. Hozumi, and V. Pirotta. Organization of immunoglobulin genes. *Cold Spring Harbor Symp. Quant. Biol.* 42 (1977): 921–31.

Certain parasites escape their host's defenses by rearranging their genes.[19] Trypanosomes have surface proteins. An infected host raises an immune reaction that kills most of the parasites. The infection seems to have died down, but then it reappears. Each cycle of the disease is due to the emergence of a population of parasites with a new surface protein. This is accomplished by a rearrangement of just those genes for surface proteins. The genetic change is a rare event, but the individual parasite that undergoes the change has such an enormous advantage over the others that it will reproduce in the host until the host responds with immunity to the new surface protein.

We know now that many genetic mutations are not due to simple base changes in the DNA, as is the case with sickle cell anemia. It is common for long pieces of DNA to be found interrupting genes, presumably the result of a transposable genetic element.

Using modern molecular methods, transposable genetic elements have been isolated and characterized. Their ability to move about the genome has been the basis for their use as vectors to introduce foreign genes into fruit flies.[20] The transposable element is spliced to the gene of interest and the recombinant molecule injected into an early embryo. The movable element helps the other gene jump into the fly's chromosomes and thus become an integral and permanent part of the animal's genes.

Certain viruses resemble transposable elements, and almost certainly the two are related in evolution. These viruses transform cells the way that transposable elements enter chromosomes.

When one considers the plasticity of genes exemplified by movable elements, it is not surprising that evolution of organisms could occur either in great leaps (called punctuated evolution) or gradually as Darwin first envisaged.

---

[19] P. T. Englund, S. L. Hajduk, and J. C. Marini. The molecular biology of trypanosomes. *Ann. Rev. Biochem.* 51 (1982): 695–726.

[20] See note 7, above.

Differential gene expression (gene activation)

The direct gene product is actually RNA, not protein as I implied in the first lecture. One of the great discoveries in the past ten years has been the elucidation of the chemistry and many of the molecular details of gene expression. In a eukaryotic cell, the genes are in the nucleus where they synthesize RNA, a process called transcription. The RNA is then processed by several steps before it moves to the cytoplasm to impart genetic instructions for protein synthesis. The ultimate expression of a gene can be controlled at any one of the many steps between formation of the gene product RNA and the final production of a functional protein molecule in the cytoplasm.[21] For example, RNA is synthesized from certain genes at extremely high rates. Many RNA copies are made from these genes while even neighboring genes might be entirely silent. This is called transcriptional control. For example, in blood cells the genes for the protein globin are actively transcribed into RNA; in skin cells these same genes are silent.

The RNA that is transcribed from a gene directly is not itself usable for the formation of protein; it must be processed. The molecule requires essential modifications at each end (a cap and a tail). In addition, the RNA molecule must have certain regions removed from inside it. This is because the gene itself is interrupted by long stretches of DNA, called intervening sequences or "introns," which have no known function. These extra DNA stretches interrupt the coding order of DNA bases. In order to translate the resultant RNA into protein, these extra bases must be removed and the adjoining parts of the molecule rejoined. In some genes, there are as many as fifty interruptions of the gene, all of which must be repaired in the RNA copy. It is perhaps a testimony to the limitations of traditional genetics that scientists had no hint whatsoever of this striking and pervasive phenomenon

[21] J. E. Darnell, Jr. The processing of RNA. *Sci. Am.* 249 (1983): 90–100.

until the advent of molecular genetics. The discovery was completely empirical; it was not predicted, and we are now about eight years after the discovery with no adequate explanation for why most genes in animal and plant cells should be split by what appears to be extraneous DNA.[22] Biology is surely an experimental, not a theoretical science. Even though we do not know the purpose of what seems to be a gratuitous phenomenon, each added complexity of a system represents yet another step at which a gene might be controlled. In a few cases, RNA splicing has already been implicated in gene control. For example, two different proteins can be fashioned from the same gene just by splicing the RNA transcript differently.[23] Alternatively, synthesis of RNA can proceed from two different starting sites next to the gene with quite different efficiencies.[24] This can happen in different tissues. There are regions at the ends of genes that influence RNA synthesis. These are all control sites for differential gene function that have already been shown to play some role in the control of gene action.

The RNA message that carries genetic instructions to the cytoplasm of cells can undergo controlled metabolism. In some cases, RNA stability depends upon the presence of hormones. We began studying an exaggerated example of gene control in the silk worm about twelve years ago. Silk consists essentially of two kinds of protein molecules that are synthesized at the end of larval development by an enormous gland. The silk protein itself is virtually the only protein made by the posterior end of the silk

[22] R. Breathnach, P. Chambon, L. A. Klobutcher, and F. H. Ruddle. Organization and expression of eucaryotic split genes coding for proteins. *Ann. Rev. Biochem.* 50 (1981): 349–83.

[23] T. R. Broker, L. T. Chow, A. R. Dunn, R. E. Gelinas, J. A. Hassell, D. F. Klessig, J. B. Lewis, R. J. Roberts, and B. S. Zain. Adenovirus-2 messengers — an example of baroque molecular architecture. *Cold Spring Harbor Symp. Quant. Biol.* 42 (1977): 531–53.

[24] O. Hagenbuchle, M. Tosi, U. Schibler, R. Bovey, P. K. Wellauer, and R. A. Young. Mouse liver and salivary gland α-amylase mRNAs differ only in 5' non-translated sequences. *Nature* 289 (1981): 643–46.

gland in the last several days of larval life. Each silk gene makes about 10^4 molecules of RNA during this period, and each molecule of RNA then is responsible for the synthesis of about 10^5 molecules of silk protein.[25] That is, one gene, 10^4 RNAs, 10^9 protein molecules. We refer to this as "translational amplification" to distinguish it from gene amplification; it happens when one gene takes over the cell's metabolism. These exaggerated examples of specialized gene expression often result in the death of the cell.

There are other examples of control at the level of protein synthesis and degradation. For example, some proteins are first synthesized in a precursor form called "polyproteins."[26] Some of these polyproteins are precursor to more than one functional protein. Metabolized in one way a polyprotein yields a hormone, and in another way a different protein.

Some genes are organized into multigene families comprising more than one copy of a gene per cell. In the case, mentioned earlier, of the 5S RNA genes that encode a ribosome component, there are tens of thousands of copies of the same gene in each cell.[27] The purpose of having many identical genes is to make more of one product.

Another kind of multigene family includes genes for related but not identical genes. Well-studied examples include transfer RNA genes and histone genes. The related genes are often clustered on chromosomes. Clustered related genes occur often enough that one is led to suspect some important functional reason for the clustering. Alternatively, clustering may just mark the evolutionary origin of a gene family by a process of gene duplication and divergence.

[25] Y. Suzuki, L. P. Gage, and D. D. Brown. The genes for silk fibroin in *Bombyx mori. J. Mol. Biol.* 70 (1972): 637–49.

[26] D. F. Steiner, W. Kemmler, H. S. Tager, and J. D. Peterson. Proteolytic processing in the biosynthesis of insulin and other proteins. *Fed. Proc.* 33 (1974): 2105–15.

[27] See note 15, above.

Another example of a multigene family is the genes for blood proteins in humans. Closely related but different genes are expressed in blood cells of embryos, fetuses and adults.[28] In humans, these genes are located next to each other on one chromosome in the exact order that they are expressed chronologically in human development. We do not know if this is a coincidence or has some regulatory purpose.

DNA signals

Consider that tens of thousands of different genes are linked together in gigantic continuous molecules of DNA called chromosomes. As many as 10^8 pairs of the four bases comprise each of these giant DNA molecules. It is evident that there must be signals that identify the beginning and end of each gene. Molecules must be present in cells that will recognize these signals and instruct specific genes to make RNA while other genes remain silent. The situation is not unlike an intercontinental highway with exits and entrances for each city along the way. A road map is needed and some identifications to aid the driver who has a specific destination. Otherwise, the pavement looks the same from beginning to end. The order of the four bases in DNA not only encodes the exact order of amino acids in protein but also contains these signals. The signals are read by molecules in the cell, probably proteins. Modern molecular methods have provided enormously powerful tools to identify the DNA signals as well as the molecules that interact with the signals. This kind of research is aptly called biochemical, *in vitro*, or surrogate genetics. It is genetics that avoids the traditional methods of breeding organisms and selecting progeny for inherited traits. Instead, the purified gene is isolated by recombinant DNA methods, mutated in the test tube, and each mutant gene reisolated in pure form. One needs an

[28] E. F. Fritsch, R. M. Lawn, and T. Maniatis. Molecular cloning and characterization of the human β-like globin gene cluster. *Cell* 19 (1983): 959–72.

assay for gene function that also works in the test tube. Alternatively, the mutated gene is reintroduced into a living cell or even into a developing embryo to test whether the gene can still function properly. By systematic mutation and testing, the DNA signals of many genes have been discovered and some of the regulatory molecules in cells have been isolated.

I cannot go into detail here about these kinds of experiments. My purpose is to emphasize what can now be done with new genetic methods. These kinds of experiments were unimaginable even a few years ago, and now they are routine.

What are we going to learn about gene expression through these very powerful methods? As I mentioned, we are already learning about the exact signals in and around genes that control them and about the molecules that interact with these signals. We are beginning to understand the basis of hormone action as it affects genes. It is almost certain that many hormones work by turning genes on or off. We will learn how multiple genes are coordinated in their activity. It is evident that many genes must function together to enable a complex cell to fulfill its exact physiological roles. We are going to understand how molecules are placed in space; for example, the structure of an egg is important because molecules placed in exact locations will end up in specific regions of a developing embryo and influence development of just those cells. These carefully localized molecules commit a region of the embryo to develop in a certain way, presumably by interacting specifically with certain genes according to a precise timetable. We will learn about this in very great detail. We can expect to understand how one cell in an embryo, or in a tissue, instructs a neighboring cell and the molecular basis of such intercellular communication.

However, there are many problems we are not going to be able to solve using this methodology. Although we may understand how genes are controlled in development, paradoxically this will not tell us exactly what they do. For example, there are genes that control other genes. These genes account for the very complicated, integrated patterns that we see in tissues — the formation of wings, legs, and other complex body parts. Mutations in these genes can cause whole tissues to change. An antenna becomes a leg. One body segment changes into another. Such genes, called homeotic genes, can and have been isolated, sequenced, and characterized. We will learn about the RNA molecules which are made from these genes and even about the proteins encoded by them. We can determine many things about a protein, such as its physical characteristics, its cellular location, and the other molecules in cells that the protein interacts with. But how do these facts explain how an antenna or a leg is made? What is "legness" anyway? These are concepts which elude us. In our pursuit of them we are going to be helped immeasurably by modern genetic methods, but they are not going to be elucidated entirely by existing methods. We will need more biology, biophysics, and biochemistry and a whole new set of principles and methods before we discover these greater global concepts and learn how embryos develop.

Of Human Freedom

GEORG HENRIK VON WRIGHT

THE TANNER LECTURES ON HUMAN VALUES

Delivered at
The University of Helsinki

May 16 and 17, 1984

GEORG HENRIK VON WRIGHT was born in Helsinki (Helsingførs), Finland, in 1916. He has been professor of philosophy in the universities of Helsinki and of Cambridge, and was for twelve years Andrew D. White Professor-at-Large at Cornell University. Since 1961 he has held a permanent research appointment in the Academy of Finland. Professor von Wright is Corresponding Fellow of the British Academy, Honorary Foreign Member of the American Academy of Arts and Sciences, and Honorary Fellow of the Finnish Society of Sciences and of Trinity College, Cambridge. His published works include *A Treatise on Induction and Probability* (1951), *Norm and Action* (1963), *The Varieties of Goodness* (1963), *Explanation and Understanding* (1971), and *Wittgenstein* (1982).

"Hundert irreleitende Bilder kommen hier zusammen, und das macht die Schwierigkeit der philosophischen Situationen aus. Wohin wir treten, wankt wieder der Boden. Die 'grossen', schwierigen Probleme der Philosophie sind es nicht etwa dadurch, dass hier ein unerhört subtiler und geheimnisvoller Sachverhalt ist, den wir erforschen sollen, sondern dadurch, dass an dieser Stelle eine grosse Zahl irreführender Ausdrucksformen sich kreuzen."

Wittgenstein[1]

I

1. It is often said that the problems of philosophy are perennial. They have been discussed throughout the ages, but never solved. This is sometimes interpreted as a sign that in philosophy there is no progress or even that the pursuit of philosophers is fruitless, all in vain.

It is not *quite* true that philosophical problems are perennial. At least their place in the discussion — whether central or peripheral — is shifting. Such shifts often reflect profound changes in the intellectual culture of an era. An example is the problem of the existence of the material or outer world. Another is the problem of "the freedom of the will." The first can hardly be said even to have existed in ancient and medieval European thought. Greek philosophy was not much absorbed in discussion of the

---

[1] "A hundred misleading pictures come together here and *this* makes for the difficulty of the philosophical situations. Wherever we put our feet, the ground yields. The 'great', difficult problems of philosophy are this not because of the existence of some extremely subtle or mysterious state of affairs which we have to ascertain, but because in this place a great number of misleading forms of expression are crossing each other." From an unpublished work by Wittgenstein called *Bemerkungen II*.

second. Both problems got their characteristic modern twist under
the impression of the mechanistic world-view which emerged from
the revolutions in astronomy and physics in the late Renaissance
and Baroque periods. They can be said to have "crystallized" in
the philosophical system of Descartes.

It *is* true, I think, that philosophical problems are not "solved."
It sounds absurd to say that G. E. Moore (eventually) "proved"
that there exists a world external to my mind — even if one cannot find any fault with Moore's argument. At most Moore succeeded in cutting the discussion short for some time, but one can
be sure that it will be revived. One can *not* be sure, however, that
it will always be thought important. It may even come to be considered no "problem" at all (any longer).

An important aspect of change in philosophy concerns the way
its problems are formulated. The problem of freedom which is
the topic of these lectures is a good example. For a long time it
was customary to think that human actions as overt manifestations
of behaviour are caused by something called volition or acts of the
will. Human freedom, it was then often said, just consists in this:
that an agent's actions are determined by his will and not by external forces over which he has no control or power. This was
a way of reconciling freedom with determinism (cf. below, 152).
It was thought important as long as science nourished and sanctioned a deterministic world-view. But a difficulty was lurking in
the background.

Granted that action is free when in conformity with our will,
what then of the will itself? Are we free to will what we will?
Or is the will determined by something else? If the will is not
free, action determined by the will can be free at most in some
relative sense, it seems.

Questions such as these constitute what I propose to call the
"classical" problem of the Freedom of the Will. I think it is right
to say that this particular problem is now gradually receding into
obsolescence.

There is no such thing as "mere" willing. Willing has an object, is *of* something. And the same holds for intending, wanting,
and wishing. Only seldom do we explain an action by saying that
we willed or wanted just it. Giving this answer is more like brush-
ing the question of why we did it aside — like saying "it is none
of your business to inquire into the motives for my action." The
reason why I did something might be that I coveted or wanted
something else to which I thought the action conducive. This other
thing was then the object of my will. Willing *it* was the *reason*
for my action, that which made me do what I did.

The "classical" way of posing the problem of freedom can be
said to obscure the factors which are normally said to determine
our actions, viz., the *reasons* we have for performing them.

After these remarks I shall say nothing more here about the
traditional Freedom-of-the-Will problem.

There is a second way of posing the problem of freedom which
also deserves the epithet "classical," chiefly because it too is related
to traditional ideas about determinism in science. It is as follows:

Every human action has what may be termed a *physical* (bodily, somatic) *aspect* consisting in muscular activity or tension and
movements of various limbs and, through this, usually also effect-
ing some changes in the physical environment. This bodily aspect
of an action is an event, or sequence of events, in nature, i.e., in
space and time. Such events presumably have causes in the neural
system, in what one calls innervations of the muscles. The innervations may in turn be caused by antecedent somatic changes, perhaps due to stimuli from outside the body. If all natural events
are caused by antecedent natural events, going back maybe in an
infinite chain to "the dawn of creation," are not then the bodily
aspects of our actions predetermined in a way which is irrecon-
cilable with the purported freedom of the agent in relation to
what he does? This was the question which worried Kant, in particular. As a child of his times Kant did not doubt the universal
validity of the Law of Causation for the phenomenal world of

events in space and time. But man as agent, he thought, is also a citizen in the noumenal world of "things in themselves" and, as such, free and responsible for his actions. However, if the bodily life of man is governed by "iron laws" of causal necessitation, how can it happen that his limbs, on the whole, move in a way which "corresponds" to the agent's free actions? The question is obscure. The way to answer it is, I think, to try to formulate it clearly — and then see that there is no question at all to be answered. I shall call this the Problem of Congruence, adopting a term suggested by Professor Frederick Stoutland,[2] and I shall address myself to it in the second lecture.

2. An aspect of what it is to be free is that one is able to, can do, various things. It is therefore natural to approach the problem of human freedom from considerations about ability and its opposite, inability. My starting point will, in fact, be the latter.

Suppose a man is asked whether he can do a certain thing and answers No, he cannot do it. What could be his grounds for this answer? There are several possibilities:

I cannot drive a motorbike — I never *learnt* to do it, I do not *know how* to do it. I cannot solve this or that problem — it is *too difficult* for me; I doubt whether I could ever acquire the needed skill. I cannot buy myself a new car — I have not got the financial *means*. I cannot park here — one is not *allowed* (supposed) to do so. I cannot let you in — I am not entitled to, have *no right* to do so. I cannot eat intestines — I feel so strong an *aversion* to them. I cannot see this play in Helsinki — there is no *opportunity*. I cannot come tomorrow — I have *no time*. I cannot answer the telephone — my broken leg *prevents* me from getting out of bed.

---

[2] In his paper "Philosophy of Action: Davidson, von Wright, and the Debate over Causation," in *Contemporary Philosophy: A New Survey*, G. Fløistad, ed., vol. 3 (The Hague: Martinus Nijhoff, 1982), pp. 45–72.

If I cannot do a certain thing because I have not learnt or do not know how to do it, my inability usually pertains to an action of a certain kind or type which I cannot perform. I shall call such action *generic* and contrast it with the *individual* action I perform or omit on a given occasion. When on the other hand I cannot do a certain thing because I am prevented or have not got the means needed for doing it, my inability pertains to the individual performance of an action of a kind I am able to do. In such cases I both can and cannot do the thing in question. I cannot do it *now*, but could have done it, had it not been for this or that, since it is an action of a *kind* I can do. It makes no sense to say that I am prevented from doing something now if it is a question of something which I do not know how to do. Similarly, it is nonsense to say that I could do something if only I knew how to do it. But to say that I would do it is not nonsense. Generally speaking: *inability* to perform an individual action presupposes ability to perform the corresponding generic action.

Does ability to perform an individual action, too, require ability to perform the action generically? One must be cautious with the answer. Sometimes one succeeds in doing something, e.g., hitting a target, which one would not claim to be able to do "in general." One was "lucky." Or, the circumstances made the task easy. The case was exceptional. Normally, however, what I can do on the individual occasion is an action *of a kind* which I can do.

It seems, therefore, that of the two "cans" the generic is primary. One could even reserve the term "ability" for it. One could then contrast "the can of ability" with "the can of successful performance." This is, for some purposes, useful terminology.

What *is* it to be able to perform an action? The way to tackle the question is to ask: When do we *say*, in colloquial language, that a person *can* perform an action of a certain kind or type, for example jump across a certain ditch without wetting his feet in the water? We say this, if normally or on most occasions when he undertakes to do the action he succeeds in performing it. Instead of "undertakes to do" we could say "chooses to do" or "sets himself to do"; occasionally also, depending upon the nature of the action, "tries to do."

But could one not sometimes say truly of a person that he can do an action of a certain kind even though he never tried or never did it? Yes — provided the action is sufficiently like another generic action for which his ability is already established. Perhaps our man never jumped this very ditch, or any ditch at all, but was good at athletics. Then, offhand, he may be pronounced able to perform this special trick too.

What about actions which are such that an agent *always* does them? Normally, if I can do an action of a certain type I do it on *some* occasions which afford an opportunity for doing it, and do not do (omit) it on others. Some actions, however, may be such that I do them whenever I have an opportunity. Then there usually is a reason why I always do them — for example that doing them gives me enormous pleasure, or that I am under an obligation to do them. Perhaps the action is one for the doing of which there is not often an opportunity — like going to see a play which is performed at long intervals in the place where I live. If, however, for no particular reason I always, whenever there is an opportunity, do something which I have learnt to do, do it quasi "automatically," "mechanically," one may begin to wonder whether this is still "free action" (below, p. 118). One would perhaps say that doing it has become an "obsession" with me, or call it an illness (for example kleptomania). Actions which I have learnt how to do but from which I cannot abstain are more like "reflexes" than "actions" of mine. (Generically they remain, of course, types of *action.*) They are *reactions*, one could also say, to the *stimuli* provided by the opportunities for doing them.

The "contrary" of performing an action is to omit (performing) it. Actions which one is not able to perform one also cannot omit. One is "compelled" or "forced" to leave them undone because of one's inability — but this does not mean that one "omits" them. That is: I shall use the term "omit" here in such a way that ability to omit logically presupposes ability to do.

Can one also be unable to omit an action? Surely. This is but another way of saying that one *must* (is *compelled* to) perform it. (Except when it means that one is [also] unable to perform it — but this would be an awkward use of "unable to omit.") Different cases may here be distinguished:

I cannot omit an individual action which I am, as we say, physically compelled to do. What is this? Someone grabs my arm and makes it go through certain motions, perhaps thereby emitting a signal. I try to resist but I cannot; I am too weak. Was my arm going through those movements the performance of an action by me? I think we must answer "No." The action was by the person who moved my arm, not by me. This type of "physical compulsion" is better termed "violence." One cannot, strictly speaking, be physically compelled to perform an action or, physically prevented from omitting it, which means the same. But one can be physically prevented from performing an action — for example by somebody who grabs my arm and keeps it steady when I am about to move it. Then one is physically compelled to omit its performance.

Physical prevention must be understood to mean prevention from performing an individual action which the agent would have performed on the occasion in question had he not been prevented. Perhaps he sets himself to act and recognizes the obstacle only in the course of his attempted performance. Or the obstacle occurs in the course of his attempt. Or it was there before the action was attempted and the agent knew of it and, therefore, omitted the action which otherwise he would have performed. If, however, the agent had *not* attempted the action, regardless of whether or not there was an obstacle to its performance, we do not say that he was prevented, or that his freedom was, on that occasion, restricted.

A genuine case of inability to omit (compulsion to do) is when one acts under the influence, as we say, of an irresistible desire or temptation or under a fearsome threat. "I cannot stand this smell, I must turn away." "I could not refuse handing him my wallet at gunpoint." Someone retorts that I could have let myself be shot, or, speaking of the smell, could have controlled myself. Could I really? To agree that I could not (have omitted the action) seems like saying that what I did was not "really" an action of mine, but more like a "reflex" or behaviour under physical compulsion. But if my behaviour was not just a scream or a jerk or a turning away from something but was a thing which I "knew how to do" or the significance of which I had learnt, then what I did was surely also an *action* of mine.

A further case of inability to omit is when one has to or must do something in order to attain a set end or ought to do something, because it is one's acknowledged duty. Although one often, without distorting things, says of such actions that one cannot omit them, it is also clear that normally one would not speak of compulsion in connection with them. A set end is something freely chosen, and an acknowledged duty is something one freely assents to. Both exist as the result of an agent's *self-determination*. This also holds good when what is acknowledged as duty conforms to the customs and traditions or is prescribed by the legal order of a society (cf. below, p. 118f).

3. If by ability we understand the "generic can" then one can say that the *range of freedom* of an agent is greater or smaller depending upon the number of kinds of actions he can do. This is why education: learning to do things, acquiring the appropriate know-how, is a factor which enhances human freedom. To keep people in ignorance, to deprive them of opportunities of acquiring skills and improving them through training, is thwarting freedom.

Freedom in this sense could also be called *potential* freedom. To be free (able) to do or omit an individual action can, by contrast, be called *actual* freedom. It follows from what has already been said that actual *non*freedom is a restriction upon an existing potential freedom: the agent *cannot*, on the individual occasion, do something which, in the generic sense, he *can* do. The agent's actual freedom, therefore, is greater or lesser depending upon the number of restrictions which there are on his (existing) potential freedom.

Such restrictions can be *external* or *internal*. Restrictions of either kind, moreover, are either *preventive* or *compulsive*. The members of the second pair are interdefinable. To be compelled to act is to be prevented from omitting an action — and to be compelled to omit (forbear, abstain) is to be prevented from doing (acting).

External restrictions on freedom I shall divide into *physical* and *normative* (or *deontic*). I have already argued (p. 114) that whereas one can be by physical obstacle prevented from doing various things — as, for example, a chained prisoner from escaping — and thus compelled to forbearance, one cannot rightly be said to be physically compelled to do anything, and therefore one cannot be physically prevented from forbearing anything either. This is a noteworthy asymmetry inherent in the concept of free action.

External normative restrictions on an agent's freedom are those prohibitions of a legal or moral character which are instituted in the social order, or orders, to which the agent belongs. Let it be observed in passing that the term "prohibition" is normally applied to *actions* which it is forbidden to perform. Prohibitions apply symmetrically to *omissions* too, however, in which case they are more commonly called "obligations." (Prohibition to do = obligation to omit doing; obligation to do = prohibition to omit.)

Internal restrictions on freedom can be divided into *psychological* and *normative* (*deontic*). By the first I understand "mental forces" such as desire and temptation, fear or aversion which, as the saying goes, either "irresistibly" compel us to some actions or constitute "insurmountable" hindrances to our embarking upon them. Psychological compulsion (for example acting under a threat) can sometimes come to resemble physical compulsion in that it is questionable whether the compulsory behaviour should be classified as an "action" (cf. above, p. 114). If we come to think that it cannot be thus regarded we do not impute responsibility for it to the agent. That is: we do not regard him as "free" or as an "agent" in relation to this particular behaviour. But not every case of which it is correct to say "he could not abstain" or "he could not bring himself to act" is of this character. Most cases are not, and of those which are it would be better to say that the notions of omitting and acting are no longer applicable to them.

If psychological compulsion and prevention relates to a *generic* action, then it annihilates ability and does not count as a restriction on existing potentialities of the agent. In the case of compulsion this means that the agent always, whenever there is an opportunity, does the action. He never omits it. This kind of compulsion which annihilates ability (to omit) is like an illness or an obsession which seizes an agent after he has once learnt to do a certain thing. Prevention which annihilates ability (to do) is more common. It is usually spoken of as "inhibition." The agent simply cannot bring himself to do a certain kind of action. Maybe he once upon a time was able to perform it, but later acquired an "insurmountable aversion." Then he not only never performs the action any more; he also no longer omits performing it. He *cannot do* it, and therefore he *cannot omit* it either (cf. above, p. 114).

Internal normative restrictions on an agent's freedom are the prohibitions which the agent acknowledges as his duty to observe. They can also be called self-imposed restrictions. But it should be noted that many such duties are societal norms which the agent has *internalized*, i.e., adopted as ultimate reasons for his actions and abstentions. This means that he observes the prohibitions, *because* he thinks he ought to and not, for example, because he is anxious to avoid getting into trouble with the norm-authorities. It may be suggested that *all* self-imposed duties (prohibitions, obligations) are, in fact, internalized norms of "external" origin. Duties which the agent has, so to speak, "invented" for himself are not "real" duties but *decisions* or *resolutions* of his to adopt a rule for his personal conduct. Some such rules would be like *habits* (for example, always to go for a walk before dinner).

4. Perhaps no man is "absolutely" free in the sense that he is never compelled to do or to abstain from doing anything which, in the generic sense, he can do. But let us stop for a moment to consider what such a "free" man, if he existed, would be like.

He would, first of all, never meet with any physical obstacle which prevents him from doing something which he can, i.e., has learnt or knows how to do, should he choose to do it. That such is the case might be a matter of luck with this man — but it could also be due to either an instinctive or a reasoned avoidance of the obstacles on his part.

Second, he would be so constituted that no temptation is ever "irresistible," nor any aversion or inhibition so strong that he cannot overcome it.

Third, he would never feel compelled to act under the pressure of norms. This means two things. One is that he would never observe a prohibition prescribed by some authority because he feared the consequences of refusing to obey. The second is that he would never consider it his unconditional duty to obey any rule, either self-imposed or given.

Strength to overcome aversions and resist temptations may be regarded as praiseworthy features of a man's character and also as a mark of "freedom." But what shall we think of a man whose actions are never strictly bound by norms? He is perhaps not praiseworthy. But is he even free?

In trying to answer this question we should note that refusal to let oneself be compelled to follow rules does not preclude one's actions from being in accordance with the legal and moral and other norms of society. The agent may never be in a position where he has reason to trespass — or if he comes to be in such a position he may have an even stronger overriding reason for acting in conformity with the norm. But he would never feel "bound" by the norm, either in the sense that he feels compelled to bow to the norm-authority's will, or in the sense that he makes obedience to the norm his self-imposed duty.

Norm-authorities have sometimes thought that the "true freedom" of their subjects consists in action conforming to the norms. It has also been thought that only action in conformity with self-imposed duty is "truly free."

Ideas like these need not be sheer nonsense or hypocrisy. One can try to support them by rational arguments. Such arguments would have to be conducted in axiological rather than in deontological (normative) terms. A norm provides the person to whom it is addressed with a reason for acting in a certain way. Reasons, however, can be rated as better or worse. One could make the goodness of the reasons a measure of the degree of freedom of the action. If one wants to argue that true freedom consists in norm-bound action, one would have to argue that the reasons provided by norms of a certain kind, be they the laws of the state or the laws of our moral consciousness, are *the best reasons* on which a man can act. The pros and cons of such arguments, however, will not be examined in these lectures.

5. It is often thought that the sign that an action was performed freely is that it could have been omitted — and, reciprocally, that an omission was free if the agent could have performed the omitted action. Whenever I can say truly "I could have acted otherwise" what in fact I did I did freely.

No doubt this idea touches the core of human freedom. We have no reason to doubt its *truth*. But we have, I think, great difficulties understanding precisely what it *means*.

In the justly celebrated chapter on free will in his book *Ethics*, Moore suggested that "I could have done otherwise" means that I should have done otherwise had I chosen to do otherwise.[3] Thereby he drove a wedge between freedom of action and freedom of choice. If my choice, too, was free I could presumably have chosen otherwise. When faced with the question of what *that* means, one thing Moore suggested was that "I could have chosen otherwise" means that I should have chosen otherwise had I chosen to choose otherwise.[4] Thereby the problem of freedom was only pushed one step back. In order to escape from an infinite regress Moore resorted to an epistemic move: I did not know for certain beforehand which choice I was going to make, and in this sense of "not knowing beforehand" it was *possible* that I should choose differently, that I *might* have chosen differently.

Moore, however, was not sure whether this wedge between freedom of action and of choice was necessary for solving his problem. He "confessed" that he could not feel certain that the truth of the statement that we could have done what we did not do was, in many cases, "*all* that we usually mean and understand by the assertion that we have Free Will." [5] Let us therefore lay aside the problem of choice and concentrate on the phrase "could have acted otherwise."

To say that I could have acted otherwise (omitted the action which I performed) is to affirm that my action was *contingent*. But in what sense was my action "contingent"?

No one would say that an action which I perform is logically necessary. So every action is, *ipso facto*, logically contingent. This is *a* sense of "could have acted differently," but hardly a very interesting one.

The statement that no action is logically necessary is not, however, as clear and uncontroversial as it may seem at first sight.

[3] G. E. Moore, *Ethics* (London: Oxford University Press, 1912), p. 131.
[4] Ibid., p. 134.
[5] Ibid., p. 135.

Given an action of a kind or type which I *can* perform, and given an opportunity for performing it, I shall, of logical necessity, either do or omit it right then. To count omission as a mode of action makes good sense. So why not also count the disjunction "do or omit" as a mode of action? This would then be a "tautologous action" which an agent will necessarily "perform," provided that he has the required ability and that the occasion provides an opportunity for exercising it. Given these prerequisites, he could *not* "act otherwise." Such actions are not "free." But they are actions of a very special kind, and it would be quite feasible to refuse to call them "actions" at all.

I have decided to do something. There is no doubt about my ability to do the thing in question. I do not reverse my decision. Nothing preventive intervenes. The opportunity is there. Is it not then, relative to these assumptions, logically necessary that I perform the action? If one is prepared to ascribe every conceivable failure to perform either to some preventive interference or to a reversal of decision ("change of mind"), the answer is "Yes." But the (logical) necessity of the action is then *relative* to assumptions which are themselves (logically) contingent. *Simpliciter* the action is a logical contingency. This is trivial. We feel instinctively that the meaning of "could have acted differently" is more interesting than this. But in what way?

Consider an action of a kind or type which I have learnt or otherwise know how to do. Then, normally, when I set myself (choose, undertake) to do it I succeed in the performance (cf. above, p. 113). However, I normally do not perform the action whenever there is an opportunity, but only sometimes. This is proof that the performance of the action is contingent — just as the fact that it is sometimes raining and sometimes not raining is proof that the fact that it is raining is contingent.

Are these facts about ability sufficient grounds for saying that an agent who on some occasion performed a certain action might also have omitted it, "could have done differently"?

One would wish to answer "No" to the question. That the action I performed was free must mean that I could *then*, on the very occasion for its performance, have omitted it. How can I know this? The fact that on some other occasion I omit the same (generic type of) action is no proof. So what does it mean that I could *then* have omitted it, acted otherwise?

The comparison with rainfall is useful here. The fact that it is ("happens to be") raining here and now is contingent by virtue of the fact that it is sometimes raining and sometimes not raining here. But this is fully compatible with the possibility that *whenever* it is raining this is due to some causes which make rainfall a (physical) necessity under natural law. Similarly, might not the fact that I sometimes do, sometimes omit, an action which I can do be compatible with the possibility that *on those occasions* when I do it I could not have omitted it — and on those occasions when I omitted it I could not have done it? If that actually were the case, would action then be free? One is tempted to say "No."

Assume that I perform the action *for some reason*. Perhaps I was fulfilling a promise. The fact that I had given the promise was the reason for my action. Or perhaps I was complying with an order or request. The fact that I had been ordered or requested to do something might then have been the reason why I did it. (Let us assume that the reasons why I acted actually are as stated. This *need* not be so, since, for example, the "real" reason why I fulfil a promise need not be that I have promised, but may be something else (cf. below, p. 139).

That an agent acted for a certain reason normally means that something was, for this agent, a reason for doing something *and* that he set himself (chose, proceeded, maybe upon deliberation) to do this thing *for that reason*. To say this is to intimate that he could, in fact, have acted otherwise. He could have neglected the reason and omitted the action. Or he could have performed the action for some other reason which he *also* happened to have. Or, finally, he could have performed or omitted the action but done this for no reason at all and not for any reason which he had. Normally, it is, as one says, "up to the agent" to act or not on given reasons. Action for reasons is *self-determined*.

But if he actually did not neglect a certain reason but acted on it, how could he *then* have acted otherwise? If the "then" is so understood that it, so to speak, "includes" the fact that he acted (for that reason), then he could, of course, not have omitted the action. One and the same occasion does not afford "logical space" both for performing and omitting one and the same action. "What is is necessary, *when it is*," as Aristotle said. Nothing *can be* otherwise from what it is. But it *could*, perhaps, *have been* different (from what it is). And this is precisely what we claim to be the case with most actions. (By insisting upon the "then" in the phrase "could have acted differently *then*" one can produce a kind of philosophical "cramp" or "frenzy" which blinds one to the distinction between "could have been" and "can be.")

But do we not sometimes say that a reason was *compelling* and that therefore I could not have acted otherwise. I, as we say, "had no choice." My freedom was restricted, the "freedom to the contrary" annihilated.

I give away a secret under torture. My reason for doing this can be that otherwise I could not have rid myself of a most horrible pain. In thus describing the reason it is presupposed that I suffered from the pain, wanted to get rid of it, and thought (or knew) that in order to achieve this I must confess the secret. The *pain* as such is no reason for my action. Its rôle is rather that of a *cause*. It "compels" or "forces" me to act for the reason mentioned. Was my action then "free," i.e., was it "up to me" to act or not to act in the way I did? The question can only be answered by considering a wider context than just this one occasion. If, on some other occasion or maybe several other occasions I could withstand (in all appearances) an equal or maybe even greater pain, then we would (probably) think of my action as free. One would say that I *can* withstand a pain of this intensity — "can" meaning

now that I have the required *ability* (the generic "can do" mentioned above, p. 113). This being so, it was still "up to me" to act
on the "compelling" reason; my confession was a product of my
self-determination. I could have acted otherwise. But if I am
notoriously bad at standing pain, the case may be judged differently. Not necessarily, however. Other persons are known to have
withstood even greater pain; some to have let themselves be tor-
tured to death. Am I sufficiently unlike them to warrant the
judgement that I could *not* have acted differently? The answer
would depend upon further facts about me (and about those more
heroic people). Maybe a sufficient number of such facts are known
or can be ascertained so as to enable us to answer the question one
way or the other. But it may also be that a factual basis for a well-
grounded answer cannot be established. Then we simply cannot
tell (decide) whether my action was free, whether I could have
acted differently, whether it was "up to me" to perform or omit
the action.

I got frightened by a bull and screamed. If I screamed in order
to call for help or in order to frighten away the bull, I acted for a
reason. I could then also have suppressed the scream and done
something else instead. But a scream of fright can be "automatic,"
"mechanical," "uncontrollable," "a reflex." Then my reaction,
screaming, is not an action. And there surely are such "primordial"
reactions of fright — and also of delight.

Sometimes an agent performs an action *for no particular reason*. We agree it was an action; it was not done "by mistake."
Let us also assume that the action is of a kind which the agent does
not always do, whenever there is an opportunity, "mechanically,"
like a reflex. So, in a sense his performance was contingent; he
might not have done it just then, on that occasion. But does saying that he could, on that occasion, have acted differently now
mean anything over and above that we do not know why he did
the thing in question then (nor does he), but we know (and so
does he) that on some occasions he does it, on others not? It does

not make much sense to say that he was free or that he was not free to act differently *on that very occasion*. And this is so just because his action had no reason, was "fortuitous." If, however, what he did was something annoying or obnoxious we might ask him to "control" or "watch" himself better in future — and thereby we should give him a *reason* for *not* doing the thing in question "for no particular reason" on other occasions.

Cases of fortuitous actions are perhaps not very frequent. But assume that they become very frequent with an agent with regard to one or several types of action. He quite often does certain things without deliberating beforehand and without being able to connect them with any reason when challenged to reflect on them in retrospect. He cannot account for these actions of his. Can he be held "responsible" for them? Was he *"free"* to do or omit them? Shall we perhaps after all classify them with "reflexes" rather than with "actions"? Such questions may be interesting to consider — sometimes because they challenge questions of sanity and mental illness — but one should resist a temptation to "force" a clearcut answer to them.

To sum up: The phrase "could have acted otherwise," i.e., "could have omitted what was done or done what was omitted" has not one but several (related) meanings. In the weakest sense the phrase is true of anything which can truly be called an action (or omission) and means simply that the performance and omission of actions are logical contingencies. In a stronger sense the phrase is true of the performance and omission of any (normal) action which the agent is able (has learnt to, knows how) to perform or omit. Then it means that there are occasions when the agent performs the action and other occasions when he omits it. In a still stronger sense the phrase is true when an agent *for some reason* performs (omits) an individual action of a type which he is (generically) *able* to perform but also to omit. Then the action (omission) springs from the self-determination of the agent. Of a good many such actions, however, the phrase "could *not* have acted differently," is *also* true — meaning that the reason which prompted the action was, as we say, compelling. Then the freedom of the agent was restricted. In marginal cases the restriction is so severe that we judge it impossible for the agent to have acted otherwise. This happens when we, usually on the basis of experience of analogous occasions, would deny that the agent has the *ability* to omit that which on this individual occasion he did. In cases, finally, when an action takes place apparently for *no* reason we sometimes look for (physical) causes and hesitate to call the behaviour (full-fledged) "action." Our attitude will then depend on the frequency and character of such "fortuitous" behaviour — and on how we evaluate it morally. It is doubtful whether we should call such actions "free" *when they occur*.

6. Normally, we said (above, p. 123), it is "up to the agent" *whether* he will act for such and such reasons which are there for him to act upon, or not.

But is it also "up to the agent" to have the reasons which he happens to have? If "up to the agent" means that the agent could choose, on a given occasion, which reasons to *have* for his action, the answer is "No." Such a choice simply makes no sense. But if the phrase means that he, normally, can choose which reasons to *act upon* (among those he has), the answer is "Yes."

The reasons for acting which an agent has, on a given occasion, are often "given" to him independently of his own (previous) action. An order could be an example — but also something "internal" such as a sudden wish to take some physical exercise or listen to music.

A man wants and shuns, likes or desires, hates or fears certain things and he knows, or thinks he knows, ways of securing for himself what he wants and avoiding what he shuns. By virtue of this he has (gets) reasons for and against certain actions of his. He has, moreover, been brought up to know what is expected of him in various situations and he has been placed, or has placed himself, in positions connected with duties and rights in relation to his fellow human beings. His involvement in the social fabric constantly provides him with reasons for and against certain actions.

The existence of reasons for a man to act in certain ways are facts about him. They are not *his* makings in the same sense as his *actions for such and such reasons* can be said to be his makings, i.e., result from his self-determination. But the majority of reasons an agent has for his actions are there as the result or consequence of human action, including actions of the agent under consideration himself. Things have been done to him; he has for example been given a certain education and training or, on the contrary, been excluded from education and training. His "tastes" for various things have been cultivated, partly by others, partly by himself. He has by birth a certain place in the social order, and this place has been changed in the course of his life, partly dependent on his doings, partly independently of them. To the extent that the reasons a man has for his actions depend on his own actions in the past one may say that it has been "up to him" to have them or not.

In these facts about the reasons is reflected the way in which the range of a man's actual freedom, i.e., of things he will do if he chooses to do them, will wax and wane as a result of what happens to him or how he "builds" his own life. It is also possible to say that the *more* reasons an agent has for and against actions which he can do, the *greater* his freedom of action (choice). But greater freedom may also imply greater difficulties and uncertainty in taking decisions — and in this way freedom of choice may inhibit action.

7. The word *reason* in English refers to the rational faculties of man. A reason for action is something which, *prima facie*, it is rational or reasonable to act upon. The two adjectives, incidentally, are not used as synonyms in ordinary language. "Reasonable" carries a stronger value-load than "rational." Of some

actions which took place for a reason one would say that they were rational but not (very) reasonable.

A reason for action can also be called a *ground*. In German, a reason is called *Grund*, or sometimes *Vernunftsgrund*, which intimates a relation to the faculty of reason. In Swedish there is, in addition to the word *grund* also a word *skäl*. To both one can prefix *förnufts-* ("of the reason"). Adding the prefix in German or Swedish serves the purpose of distinguishing ground as reason from ground as cause. But the reason–cause distinction is not a clear one — neither in language nor at the level of concepts.

What then is a reason for action? One could answer that a reason is anything to which the action is an adequate response. But what does this mean?

A reason can be given to an agent in the form of a challenge the meaning or purpose of which is that the agent should react to it in a certain way. The response is expected, maybe even required or obligatory. For example: I do something. Why? The answer is that I had promised to do this thing. The person to whom I gave the promise expects this action from me; it is my duty (obligation) to him to perform it. Or, I stop my car in front of the red traffic light. Why? One is forbidden, not supposed to, drive against it.

It should be noted that the fact that a challenge makes its appearance "in the world" (a command being shouted out, the red light appearing in front of my car) is not, by itself, a reason for any action. It becomes a reason in virtue of the fact that the agent to whom it is addressed is aware of and understands (the "meaning" of) the challenge, i.e., knows how to react to it adequately. Whether he then reacts or not is another question.

The presentation of the challenge has, so to say, to be sieved through the medium of the understanding in order to become a reason for the agent.

A reason is often also present in the form of something an agent covets or wants (to be, to do, to get, to have or to promote) in combination with an opinion of his that a certain action is conducive to or otherwise useful for the attainment of his goal or "end of action." The action which takes place for that reason could be something very simple and direct like opening a window to get fresh air, or it could be something complex and remote like registering for a course in order to promote one's education.

Ends of action are often considered means to some remoter ends. Having the latter in view is then a reason for pursuing the former. The ultimate ends are things a man cherishes as good in themselves. They are his "ultimate goods" or "ultimate values," things which, as we say, give "meaning" to his life. Which they are and how a man chooses to pursue them will vary from man to man. They are not necessarily things we all agree are noble or praiseworthy.

It may be suggested that the ideally rational agent is one whose reasons for action are always anchored in ultimate ends. Perhaps no man can live up to the ideal. How many of us can tell which our ultimate ends (goods, values) in life are? But the farther towards something ultimate we can push our answers to the question *why* we undertake to do what we do, the better do our reasons for action deserve to be called rational.

If by the "apparent good" of an agent we mean all that he values as good in itself, then we could say that, ideally, a man's reasons for action should be those things which make his actions rational from the point of view of his apparent good. If, furthermore, one distinguishes between a man's apparent and his real good, one can go a step further and say that a (truly) reasonable man is one whose actions are based on care for his real good.

One may also wish to say of such an ideally reasonable man that he has attained the highest degree of freedom. But I shall not pursue here this moralistic thinking about reasons, rationality, freedom, and the good.

Sometimes we say that the reason a man has for some action of his is really *no reason* why he should do it. This can mean several things. It can mean, for example, that his opinion (belief) about the conduciveness of a certain action to a certain end is erroneous (false, "superstitious"). By making him "know better" the means–end connections we can influence his reasons and therewith also his actions. But it can also mean that what *for him* is a reason for an action would not be a reason for us; for example because we censure or disapprove of something he aspires after and wish to change his valuations — not his opinions about the means but his pursuit of ends.

8. One distinguishes between *reasons* and *motives* (for an action). Ordinary language does not uphold this distinction very clearly. Reasons are often spoken of as motives, and vice versa. One must not be pedantic about the use of the words. But some conceptual observations on the distinction may be called for.

Motives have not the same link with the rational faculties of man that reasons have. Motives can be irrational. And irrational motives can prompt a man to act perfectly rationally for reasons. I shall try to explain:

An important class of motives are constituted by "passions" such as jealousy, hatred, greed. They tend to "move" people to action; under their influence people do various things. That a man, for example, hates another man will usually manifest itself in various "ends" of action which he then pursues. He may want to inflict harm on the object of his hatred. Having such objectives is not so much a "consequence" of his passion as something "constitutive" of it; his objectives are the "criteria" on the basis of which we attribute the passion in question to him. If now a man with such objectives thinks that a certain action will be conducive to their attainment — say, harm the person whom he hates — then the fact that he has this objective and opinion will constitute a *reason* for him to do the action in question. It is of such reasons that we sometimes say that they are "no reasons" on the ground that we disapprove of the objective and of the feeling which it manifests (cf. above, p. 130). "You hate him and doing this to him would harm him, I agree; but that is no reason why you should do it. I realize that you hate him considering what he has done to you; but try to understand him and you will feel compassion for him and pity him rather than hate him."

The "good" passions are motives for action, too. Supreme among them is love. The lover will do a number of things for the reason that he considers them promotive of the happiness and well-being of the beloved. His actions are motivated by love, but one would not normally call his love a "reason" for what he does.

There are other ways, too, in which one can mark a distinction between motives and reasons. Having a reason involves *understanding* something: for example the meaning of a practice (promising, answering questions) or a causal relation between means and ends. Motives may be "blind" like sometimes love and hatred, or have an animal character like hunger and thirst.

We need not here uphold a sharp separation between motives and reasons, however. By the *motivation(al) background* of an action I shall understand the complex web of factors (motives, reasons) to which we refer when we explain why something was done or omitted or of which we say that they led to or prompted the action or made the agent act or moved him to action.

9. In a good many cases of simple actions the agent has just one reason for doing or omitting it. But in other cases the motivation background of an action is *complex*. The complexity can be either one of *number* or one of *strength* of the reasons.

The fact which I call the *complexity of the motivation* is well known to psychologists and psychoanalysts. As far as I can see, this fact has not been much noted in recent philosophical discussion of action and action-explanation. This is a limitation which we must try to overcome.

There can exist many reasons why an agent should act as he does. For example: An agent does something which he has promised to do.

But he also expects a reward or a service in return from the promisee. Would he have fulfilled his promise had he not had that expectation?

Sometimes there are reasons *for* but also *against* a certain action. (A reason *against doing* something is a reason *for omitting* it.) For example: The thing the agent had promised to do and for which he is expecting a service in return is perhaps something shady, disreputable or, maybe, even criminal. In this situation the agent has to "form a balance": he has to "weigh" the "sum total" of the reasons for and against the action. How he then acts shows which one of the (sums of) reasons was heavier (stronger).

Also among the reasons, if there are several, which are all for (or all against) an action some may be stronger than others. And the strength of a particular reason may be influenced by the presence in the motivation background of other reasons for or against the action. For example: considering the disreputable character of the act and the agent's awareness of this, the fact that he had promised was a rather weak reason why he should ("after all") do it. But the expectation of reward may have constituted, for him, such a strong reason for the action that, because of this, he did it. Maybe he did not attach any weight at all to the fact that his action was the fulfilment of a promise *as a reason for his action.* ("I know full well that promises of such acts need not be kept.") But the fact that his action was the fulfilment of a promise *and* disreputable may be highly relevant to his expectation of a reward. ("If I promise to do this shady trick for his benefit, I am sure he will reward me.")

When reasons are balanced against each other and one found heavier than another, contrary reason, the first is said to be *overriding* in relation to the second. An overriding reason is not necessarily a reason of the kind we call *compelling*, nor vice versa. A reason can be judged compelling also in the absence of any contrary reason. Often at least, in calling reasons compelling one excludes them from deliberation. They leave no choice open to the agent (cf. above, p. 124).

When, in deliberation or in retrospect, reasons are rated for strength they are often called good or bad, better and worse. But rating reasons for goodness can also be a moral evaluation of them. And a morally commendable reason for an action is often called "strong." But the strength which on moral or other grounds we attribute to reasons must be distinguished from their (actual) strength in moving agents to actions and abstentions.

10. When the motivation background is complex one can usually not point to any *one* reason when trying to explain why the action was performed or omitted. A full description of the background may be needed for the sake of understanding what took place. This description will also contain estimates of the relative strength (weight) of the reasons known to have been present. Some of the reasons for the action will be thought to have contributed more, others less to its actual performance. Some may have been completely "inefficient," others again so strong that they alone, in the absence of all the others, would have conquered, overridden, the restraining influence of possible reasons against the action. Then we say that the action was *over-determined*.

The existence of reasons for an action is an ambiguous concept. When an action is judged from "outside," i.e., by someone other than the agent himself, it is often said that there were (good) reasons why the agent should not have performed it. But the agent did not consider them. He was not aware of their presence or did not understand their significance. We sometimes blame an agent for such ignorance. "He ought to have known what this meant" (for example the hooting of a horn).

Reasons of this kind, I shall say, were *not present for the agent* (did not "exist for him") at the time of his action. They may, in various ways, be relevant to the *evaluation* (blaming or praising) of the action. But they are not relevant to its *explanation* since they do not belong to the motivation background of the action. And the same is true of those reasons which were present for the

agent, which belong to the motivation background, but which he
chose to ignore. We often blame an agent for not having taken
them into account.

Consider the following example. I am invited to a party. I
decline, giving as a reason that I have another engagement. My
reaction (declining the invitation) is a perfectly adequate response
in view of this fact. It is a valid *excuse*. But is it the reason *why*
I declined? The party would have bored me. I am shy — I hate to
be in the presence of so many people. I might have met X at the
party; I dislike him intensely; I am, in fact, afraid of meeting him.

All the things mentioned are reasons for declining the invitation. But I did not mention any of them when I was challenged
to explain why I declined. Perhaps I did not think about them
very much, since I had a valid excuse. Maybe it did not even occur
to me that I might meet X at the party. If this is *really* so, i.e., that
it did not occur to me, then the fact that I would have feared meeting him was not one of the reasons present for me. But is it quite
certain that the possibility did not "occur" to me? Surely I knew
that X is a great friend of the family to whom I was invited, that he
often visits them. Since I knew this, I *must*, "subconsciously," have
known, too, that I was likely to meet him there. Who is to tell?

We shall presently have to say more about such cases. Here
we only note the following two things. First, that it is not always
clear and easy to tell which reasons for or against a certain action
shall count as belonging to the agent's motivation background.
And second that reasons which undoubtedly belong to this background — for example that I am a shy person and do not like big
parties — do not necessarily "contribute" to my actual conduct.
It is, in other words, important to distinguish between reasons
existing for the agent and reasons influencing his action — between
existing reasons and *efficacious* reasons. An existing but not efficacious reason can serve as an *excuse* for doing something. But it is
no part of the explanation. Only of efficacious reasons do we say
that the agent acted *for those reasons* or *because* of them.

11. To explain an individual action is to answer the question why this action was performed, and correspondingly for an omission.

In its general form the formulation above covers several *types* of action explanations. The only type which will be discussed here is explanations in the terms of reasons. Such explanations I shall also call *understanding explanations*.

Another type of explanation is *medical*. An explanation of this type attributes an action, or a failure to act, to a diagnosed illness or deficiency — due perhaps to something "somatic" and thus to a "cause" rather than to a "reason." Still another kind of explanation is *sociological*. It is concerned with abilities, or the lack of abilities, rather than with individual actions. It explains, for example, why an agent can or cannot do certain things because of economic status, education, or social position.

Action explanations of the types here called "medical" and "sociological" are in a certain sense *scientific* explanations. They usually have a background in some *theory* about man or about society. Their purpose is often *to cure* an agent of some illness or to remove some hindrance to his development. Reason-giving explanations, by contrast, are not typically what we would call "scientific." The purpose they serve is usually *evaluative*. Does the agent deserve blame or praise for what he did? The answer may crucially depend upon the reasons which he had. Hence we must *understand* the action before we can *judge* the agent.

12. In giving an "understanding" action explanation it is presupposed that the action has been correctly identified as an action of a certain type and that the agent actually had the reasons mentioned in the explanation. The action and the agent's reasons are, so to speak, the facts of the case. The presupposition that they have been established, however, is not trivial (cf. below, p. 147).

What the behaviour of the agent was, or what it caused to be, may be identified as a result of a good many generic actions which, however, cannot be imputed to the agent as *his* actions. The agent's arm moved in a way constituting a signal. Did he signal? Perhaps he had not the faintest idea that he was doing such a thing. Then the action cannot be imputed to him. But if he knew the significance of the movements as a signal we can impute the action to him even if he did not "mean" (intend) to signal but meant something else, say to reach out for an object. If he did not mean to signal, he had no reason for signalling, and his action cannot be explained (understood) as that of giving a signal. We may blame him for his action ("you should have realized —"), but in order to explain it we must look for another way of identifying it. We must try to identify it as an action for the doing of which the agent had some reason(s).

Our identification of an action for the purpose of explaining (understanding) it is thus guided by what we think of as possible reasons for it. The reasons for signalling are different from those for reaching out for some object. We know, roughly, which they *are*. *Had* the agent reasons for an action of either type? He may have had for one, or for both, or for neither. If he had reasons for both, were the reasons for both efficacious? Reasons which are not efficacious do not "contribute" to the explanation, we have said (p. 135).

So our problem is: how do we identify the efficacious reasons?

To this question I shall give an answer which at first may be thought shocking. The efficacious reasons are those in the light of which we explain the action. I maintain, in other words, that one cannot separate the question of the *efficaciousness* of the reasons from the act of *understanding* the action as having been performed for those reasons. This means that the truth of the action explanation has no basis in facts *other* than the understanding itself of the action in the context of its reasons.

The obvious objection to this is that it seems to open the gates for boundless subjectivism in action explanation. Must we not be able to discriminate between understanding and *mis*understanding, when explaining an action, or at least between a *better* understanding and a less good one? What then are the criteria for making these distinctions if not some facts about the action and the reasons on which our understanding of their connection may be based?

13. Understanding something requires a subject, somebody who understands. When there is a wide consensus about how something should be understood one also talks of understanding in an impersonal, derivative, sense: "It is (commonly) understood that—."

When I say that to explain an action is to connect it in the understanding with the reasons for its performance, *whose* understanding am I then thinking of? There are two possibilities to be considered:

Understanding can be by the agent himself or by one or several "outside observers" of him and his action. In the first case we speak of the agent's self-understanding; in the second I shall talk about "outside understanding" or "understanding from outside." One could also call the two first-person and third-person understanding, respectively.

It is clear that self-understanding is, somehow, *basic* to action explanation. Normally, an agent knows what, on a certain occasion, he did, i.e., under which description(s) his action is intentional. He also knows which reasons there were for him to act. In normal cases, moreover, he knows for which reasons he acted. If we, outsiders, wish to know why the agent did what he did, the obvious way to get to know this is by *asking* him.

Of most actions, no explanation is ever required. Should the agent stop to reflect why he did a certain thing he would know the answer, and should he be asked he would give it without hesitation. Nobody would have reason to doubt it. There would be complete agreement, consensus, about the case. It is in such agreement that the "truth" of an action explanation, if an explanation be required, consists.

Many cases, perhaps even a majority of cases, when an explanation for some reason or other is required, are not cases where there is consensus — at least not initially. An outsider *wonders* why the agent did what he did. (He may also wonder which action to impute to the agent, how to identify the action. But this difficulty we now assume is solved [cf. above, p. 136]). He may know something about the agent's reasons for the action but he can also see reasons against doing an action of this kind and wonders why the agent did not *omit* it. He asks the agent and the agent's answer does not satisfy him. The case looks "suspect." There must have been some other reason why he did it and which he conceals from us, we think. Or we say that he did it, not for the reason he gave, but for another reason which we know he had.

Consider our previous example of the promise (above, p. 132). The agent had given a promise. This was a reason for doing what he did. But what he did was something shady, maybe criminal, something one ought not to do. This he presumably understood was a reason against doing it. However, by doing the thing he greatly obliged the promisee and could expect a service in return. This he obviously knew too and that gave him another ("selfish") reason for doing what he did. He says, however, that he did it because he had promised. Did he not realize that what he did was something bad? Yes, but "a promise is a promise." We are left wondering.

How shall a case like this be decided?

Perhaps the situation is quite clear. The agent is openly lying. He knows full well why he did what he did and that this was not for the reason he gave us. Then his self-knowledge need not conflict at all with the outsider's suggested explanation of his case. There is in fact consensus, although it is "tacit."

The situation need not be like this, however. The agent may, as we say, be "lying to himself," too, about his reasons (motives). He fulfilled his promise and did the shady thing because of a selfish calculation, but he does not "acknowledge" this (even) to himself. Or he honestly "misunderstands" his own action — thinking, for example, that the sole reason why he fulfilled his promise was that he had promised and not that he expected to be rewarded.

(The border between cases of "lying to others" and "lying [also] to oneself" may not be sharply distinguishable.)

On what grounds could an outsider defend his claim to understand the agent (his motives) better than the agent himself? The outsider would, for example, refer to his knowledge, presumably based on past experience, of the agent's "character." Perhaps he says: "He, the agent, *is* that kind of person who gives and fulfils promises only when this is clearly to his own advantage. The moral obligation to fulfil promises does not mean anything to him. We know this." The outsider thus views the conduct of the agent in this particular case in the broader setting of the picture we have of his character. The explanation of the action offered by the outsider is more consistent or in tune with the rest of our knowledge of the agent.

The outsider's view gets further support if it turns out to be a safe basis for predictions. "You will see: when in future he promises something he will disappoint the promisee, unless he also has a selfish motive for fulfilling the promise. He is not to be relied upon." The prophecy may fail in some cases, but if it holds in many cases this supports the explanation which the outsider offered of the particular case in which he disputed the agent's own explanation of his action.

14. In case of disagreement it may of course happen that the agent convinces the outsider that the latter has misunderstood him. The outsider is then, so to speak, "converted" to the view of the agent. This case may be quite common but also not of much interest either from a philosophical or from a psychological point of view.

Of more interest is the case in which the outsider stands by his view and tries to convert the agent to a new self-understanding.

The outsider says perhaps that the agent's lips profess that he did the action for the reason X, but in his heart he knows that he did it for the reason Y. Maybe we can convert him and make him "confess" the truth.

There is an idea that the agent must be the supreme judge, the highest authority in the matter. He and he alone can see the truth directly. The outsider's evidence for *his* explanation can only be external and indirect. Agreement with the agent's self-knowledge therefore seems the ultimate test of truth in the matter.

What kind of argumentation would the outsider resort to if he tried to convert the agent? Mere *persuasion* would not be fair. If it succeeded, i.e., led to consensus, it would be a result of "brain-washing." What is a brain-washed agent's self-knowledge worth as a testimony? Even if we do not dismiss it as completely worthless, we would hardly accord to *it* "highest authority." The highest authority is now in the hands of the outsider (the "brainwasher").

The *rational* arguments which the outsider could use would be, roughly, the same grounds and evidence on which he based his initial disagreement with the agent's professed explanation. He would, for example, try to make the agent see his present action in the setting of a larger fragment of his life-history. He would point to incidents in the agent's past which are "public knowledge" and which the agent would not deny. He would also hold up for him the image of his character which others have formed and ask the agent to ponder the facts which led to the formation of this image and to compare it with his self-image. He may warn him of his own future actions, ask him to watch himself better.

Obviously, the border between rational argumentation and "brainwashing" is not always sharp. This being so, why should we think that the "internal evidence" which the agent professes to have after a "conversion" has a privileged position in relation to truth (correctness of understanding)? Perhaps there is no good reason for thinking this at all.

Assume that a "conversion" takes place. The agent says perhaps: "I now admit that I did not do it because I had promised
but because I counted upon a service in return." Or: "The reason
why I did not go to the party was that I surmised that X was going
to be there; the appointment I had could easily have been can-
celled or changed; giving it as the reason why I declined the
invitation was pretence only." And assume that we do not challenge the sincerity of these new explanatory declarations by the
agent, but accept them.

The question of philosophic importance is now: How shall we
correctly describe the imagined situation? Shall we say that *now*
the agent sees the truth about himself? It, the truth, was always
there to be seen although hidden from the agent's sight by the
veils of his self-deception. When the veils are removed *he* sees
clearly what the outside observer had already sighted, although
the latter could not be sure of the veracity of his impression until
he had it confirmed by the agent himself? *Or* shall we say that the
agent now sees his former action in a *new* light, that his consciousness has changed, and that he has acquired a new understanding of his own past? Shall we, in other words, say that a
connection (between an action and its reasons) which was already
there has been discovered, or shall we say that a new (different)
connection has been made?

It should be noted how permeated by metaphor the talk of
"truth" is here. The truth was there to be "seen" ("in his heart"),
but it was "veiled." When the "conversion" had taken place it
was "revealed" to the agent, who, as it were, then "recognized"
his "true self."

We are in the neighbourhood of what may be called the *epis-
temology of psychoanalysis.* A psychoanalyst would perhaps speak
of a subconscious understanding by the agent's super-ego of the connection between the action and the reasons. The existence of this
connection would then be brought to the surface of the consciousness of the ego which had repressed it. But this is a metaphor too.

It is tempting to resort to such metaphors as those we mentioned. They almost "force" themselves upon us. They are good *metaphors* and when used as such may be perfectly innocuous. The danger is that their use gives birth to *conceptual* mythology and mystification. One builds a "theory" of the workings of the subconscious, a "dynamic psychology." Here the task of the philosopher sets in. It is a task of "demystification." And this means a task of trying to describe the actual situation in terms which do not mislead. This is difficult.

In order to see how misleading talk of truth can be here let us ask the following question: What is supposed to have been veiled, the agent not to have seen? And let the answer be: the connection between the action and the reason which made him perform it. But this connection had not yet been established. (Unless, of course, he lied "openly.") Because "establishing" the connection means understanding the action as having been performed for that reason. So under the veil there was in fact nothing to be seen! The object of vision was created in the very moment when the veil was lifted! What is *now* established, viz., the connection in the understanding, simply was not there *then*.

The assumption is that the agent did not lie about his reasons when first asked to explain his action. If he did not lie he was sincere. But how can he have been sincere since later he admitted that the reason was something different? Unless we wish to say that he was brain-washed we must, I think, insist that he cannot have been *quite* sincere. He was, so to speak, half sincere, half lying. How shall this state then be described?

Consider again the example of the promise. If we attribute its fulfilment to a selfish expectation by the agent, the agent must somehow have "had" this expectation at the time of the action. Otherwise we could not say truly that there existed this reason *for him* for fulfilling the promise. He must have known, for example from previous dealings with the promisee, that he was doing something for which a service in return could be expected.

Perhaps he did not think of this at the moment of his action. Maybe he felt "ill at ease" in face of the shameful thing; the thought of a service in return just "flashed" before his mind but was turned aside by the voice of conscience which said "you promised and cannot deceive your friend." This, for example, would be a description of what it is to be half-sincere when one has to explain one's action. The description shows *in which sense* the connection between the action and the selfish reason for doing it *was already* there from the beginning, albeit in an "embryonic" form, and *not only* from the moment of conversion.

It will be helpful here to warn against a temptation to *insist* upon the existence of an explanation of any action which has a complex motivation background. The complexity may not consist only in the fact that there are *many* reasons, or reasons *for* and *against*, or reasons of various *strength* (cf. above, p. 132). "Complexity" can also mean that the background is *opaque*. And here "opaque" does not signify merely that we cannot *see* through the web of motives but that the motives *are*, in fact, confused. The opaqueness is, so to speak, "ontic" and not (only) "epistemic." When we then explain the action in the setting of its reasons (motives) we actually *create* an order where before there was none.

I shall therefore say that what happens in a "conversion" of the kind which we are considering is that the agent connects in his understanding *in a new way* some action of his with the motivational background for its performance. He explains his action differently — not because new facts about its reasons have come to light but because facts already there are connected (arranged, articulated) in a new way. If this new understanding is called better, more correct or more true, than the previous one this is because it matches the broader frame of facts about the agent's past history in which the outsider had from the beginning been reviewing his present action.

In view of what has been said, what happens to the idea of the agent as supreme authority in understanding his own case (action) ?[6] I think we must say that it withers away. The conversion is not a revelation of *truth*, but a reaching of a *consensus*.

The idea of the agent's authority has, of course, a rational foundation (cf. above, p. 138). This, however, is easily misinterpreted. The agent is likely to know more facts about the case than the outsider — particularly about existing reasons for his action. Therefore the outsider who distrusts the explanation of the agent will have to elicit information from him. The keys to a new understanding of the action are thus, in the main, in the hands of the agent himself and have to be obtained from him. But as for the new understanding itself, the agent is not necessarily better equipped than the outsider. The outsider may be superior. To neither of the two belongs exclusively the right to pass a final judgement.

15. Assume, however, that no conversion takes place but that the outside observer stands by *his* explanation of the agent's action. Does this mean that the case remains undecided?

It is good to remember here that "decided" means that consensus is reached. It does not mean that the agent upon scrutinizing himself testifies to the truth in the matter.

But what is required in order that we may talk of "consensus" having been reached? Is it necessary to have the agent's endorsement of the outsider's explanation? Once we have demolished the idea of the agent's privileged position with regard to (access to) truth, the question is worth considering. It is clear that in normal cases the agent's agreement is desirable, even essential. If we come to think that his professed self-understanding can be ignored, we must have special reasons. *One* possible reason is that

---

[6] For how my opinions on this question have changed, cf. my book *The Varieties of Goodness* (London: Routledge & Kegan Paul, 1963), p. 190, and the papers "Determinism and the Study of Man" (1976) and "Explanation and Understanding of Action" (1981) reprinted in *Philosophical Papers I, Practical Reason* (Oxford: Basil Blackwell, 1983).

we are convinced that he is lying — and thus "really" agreeing with us. But this possibility we shall here ignore as being of minor interest (cf. above, p. 139). A more interesting case is when we judge the agent's character so morally corrupt or perverse that he is unable to give a coherent and honest account of the motives and aims of his actions. We simply disqualify him as a judge in his own case. Only the opinions of outsiders now count for obtaining consensus about how his actions are to be explained. And all outsiders may, in fact, agree — with the possible exception of some whose judgement we think, on independent grounds, cannot be trusted or can be ignored. Then the case is "decided."

That cases like this occur cannot be denied. But there is something tragic about them. That somebody else should have supreme authority in cases which concern my "inner life" may be thought humiliating. May not such an authority misuse his position for "brain-washing" — perhaps with a view to furthering uniformity in people's thoughts and actions? And may not this lead to the gravest injustice in treating a person? Of these dangers we have good reason to be aware — not least in the ominous year 1984.

How much easier would not things be if we could believe in an absolute truth in these matters, a truth which exists independently of what anybody thinks about the reasons for our actions? It is characteristic that those who misuse their authority when they disqualify the testimonies of the agents often do this in the name of a "higher" truth, perhaps sanctioned by "science," which the recalcitrant agent is being forced to accept. And it is also characteristic that those who resist often seek comfort in the belief that there is an "inner" truth to which they *alone* have access and which they know. The insight that there is no such truth, neither "inner" nor "outer," is the weapon with which we must try to fight both the self-righteousness of excessive subjectivity and the pretensions of false objectivity in matters of understanding human action.

16. To explain an action is a facet of understanding the agent as a *person*. The same holds for the imputation of actions to him, and for the attribution to him of reasons for actions.

One can distinguish layers of facts about an agent attributed to him in the understanding of him as a person. Facts of an inferior layer are often unquestionably taken for granted in efforts to establish facts about him on a superior level. Thus, for example, we may without question regard it as a fact that he did a certain action and also that he had such and such reasons, but be hesitant about the explanation. Did he do it for this reason or for that one? This may lead us to re-examine the already accepted facts of the inferior level. Perhaps we had mistakenly imputed to him the action, i.e., his behaviour was not intentional under the description we had first given to it.

In attributing reasons for action to an agent we normally also attribute to him various abilities, beliefs, desires and inclinations, the understanding of institutions and practices of the community, and other things which characterize him as a person. Some of these features may date far back in his life history. They constitute a kind of background or "program" which has to be assumed if certain things he did or which happened to him shall count as reasons for subsequent action (for example, that he understands a certain language). These other things, then, speaking metaphorically, are "inputs" playing on the "keyboard" of his programmed personality. His action is the "output."

However distasteful these analogies in terms of computer language may sound, I think they are useful when the problem of free action is discussed in the context of our present cultural situation. In the next lecture I shall make further use of the metaphor.

II

1. Not all actions are performed for reasons. Actions can be unintentional, done by mistake, or "for no particular reason." Some such actions shade into "reflex." If we wish to explain them

we have to look for *causes* in stimulations of the agent from inside or outside his body. From the point of view of their explanation, these actions are movements, or the inhibition of movements, of the limbs and organs of the human body.

Also, actions which take place for reasons have a "bodily aspect." As its *primary* form I shall regard overt ("visible") movements of the body or some parts of it. These movements may effect further changes outside the body. Some such effected changes are normally used for *identifying the action*, i.e., for telling *what* the agent did — for example opened a door. They are what I have called elsewhere the *results* of the action.[7] Further changes effected by the results of actions I call (causal) *consequences* of those actions.[8]

In some simple cases the overt bodily movements themselves are regarded as results of an action — for example the action of raising one's arm. But more often the bodily movements are only (causal) prerequisites of (the results of) an action. These overt prerequisites have in their turn a covert background in the tension and relaxation of muscles "inside" the body. Muscular activity again has a causal background in processes in the nervous system. In the last resort, causes for these processes may be sought in stimulations of the nervous system from outside the agent's body. In this way the causal prerequisites for (the results of) our actions may be traced back to things which took place "in the world" outside our bodies and independently of us (our actions).

Not every human action results in a change in the world. Preventive or suppressive action, if successful, results in a not-change. Such action nevertheless has a physical (somatic) aspect, the characteristic form of which is muscular tension. For example, I press my hand against a door, thus preventing it from opening when someone else is trying to push it open.

---

[7] *Norm and Action* (London: Routledge & Kegan Paul, 1963), p. 39f.
[8] Ibid.

There is a noteworthy asymmetry between *performance* and *omission* of action in relation to bodily manifestations. In the normal cases, omissions do not require any (physical) effort. They lack a somatic aspect. Omission of actions for which there existed no reasons, for or against, would hardly ever be even noticed or require an explanation. The typical quest for explanation of an omission has the form: Why did an agent not do this or that for the doing of which he had a reason and opportunity (and which he can do)? And sometimes the answer is that he was prevented by an outer or inner *physical* factor (force).

That every action (other than omission) should have a somatic aspect is, I think, a conceptual or intrinsic feature of action. One can imagine "action at a distance" — for example that people could make things move or fall to pieces just by looking at them or by pronouncing some words in a low voice. Looking too is "somatic," and so is subvocal speech. But what about the possibility of causing changes to take place by "mere" thinking or willing? What would this mean, if not some exertion of bodily effort such as frowning, clenching one's fists, closing one's eyes, compressing one's lips, etc.? One can imagine that such changes in the soma would effect changes outside the body even though in fact they do not do so. But a concept of action which is completely detached from somatic change would no longer be *our* concept of action.

I am not denying that there are *mental acts* and that some of them, such as imagining or thinking, are subject to the will. But the results of such action — if we call it by that name — are not changes and not-changes "in the world." Pure mental activity, as we know it, is therefore conceptually different from what here, in conformity with common usage, I call human action.

2. There was a time when we did not know anything about the rôle of the nervous system in relation to muscular activity and overt bodily movement. *Logically*, it is of course contingent that

there exists a causal connection between the two at all. Suppose that this connection had not (yet) been discovered, that we still lived in "blissful ignorance" of it. Would this have been relevant to the problem of freedom of action or of the will?

The question is worth asking, and in one sense of "relevant" the answer is: "Yes, probably," because it is certainly not a historical accident that the form in which the problem of free action has tormented philosophers for the last three centuries or so dates from the very time when the fundamental discoveries were made concerning the physiological mechanisms of the body, among them the nervous system. Descartes holds a key position in these developments. It was under the influence of the "new philosophy" of mechanistic determinism, the "scientific revolution" of the seventeenth and eighteenth centuries, that the problem acquired the typical form which it has retained to this very day, viz., whether one can "reconcile" the idea of free action with the idea of a strictly deterministic course of events in nature (cf. above, p. 111).

Did the problem then not exist before Descartes? In Ancient philosophy we find discussion of determinism and also of voluntary action, but not much discussion of the two in relation to one another. In the Christian philosophy of the Middle Ages our problem has a definite ancestor, the question how to reconcile the notion of man as a free agent with the existence of an omnipotent and omniscient God.

It is interesting to compare these two variants of our problem, the "theological" and the "scientific" — as they might be called. When the idea of an omnipotent and omniscient God gradually withered away, the rôle which it had exercised in the intellectual imagination of a culture was taken over by the idea of mechanistic determinism. This latter is now in its turn gradually being eroded under the influence of scientific developments. These developments too are likely to affect the form which the problem of freedom is going to assume and the rôle it is going to play in the philosophy of the future. For the time being one can only speculate about this, and we shall not do so here.

3. Philosophers may be divided into two main groups depending upon whether they regard freedom (of action) and universal determinism (in nature) as compatible with one another or not. Philosophers of the first group are said to defend a *compatibility thesis*, those of the second group an *incompatibility thesis*.

A supporter of the view that freedom is incompatible with universal determinism is facing a choice between the following two positions: Either he has to deny that the physical aspect of our actions is completely determined by antecedent physical states and natural laws, or he has to deny freedom — label free action some sort of "illusion."

Each of the two positions exists in many variants. In our century, indeterminism has sometimes been defended with arguments from microphysics (quantum theory). Physics is no longer wedded to the idea of universal determinism in the way it was in the eighteenth and nineteenth centuries (cf. above, p. 150). This is true — but the question whether indeterminism in physics is "ontic" or "epistemic" is still open to debate. If it is the latter, indeterminism in physics reflects limitations in our knowledge and is compatible with determinism in nature.

It is an old idea in philosophy that the freedom of our actions is an "epistemic illusion" due to our ignorance of their causes. This idea is related to one of Moore's suggested interpretations of "could have done otherwise" (cf. above, p. 120). Since, at least in many cases, we do not know what our choices (of course of action are going to be, we say it is possible that we are going to do a certain thing but also possible that we are going to omit the action.[9] This corresponds to a common and natural use of "possible," roughly equivalent to the phrase "for all we know." A determinist who thinks that our choices (of course of action) are, in effect, determined, would then label the idea that man is "free" to choose his actions an "epistemic illusion."

[9] Cf. Moore, *Ethics*, p. 136.

There is a "classic" defense of the compatibilist position which should be mentioned here. It enjoyed a certain popularity with writers on ethics of the former century. They thought that motives and reasons for action are (comparable to physical) causes.[10] If every action "flows" from a motive, then actions are just as rigidly determined as events in nature. But then actions spring from the agent's *self-determination* and not from external causal factors. Determinism must not be confused with fatalism.[11] Human freedom consists exactly in this, that human actions are determined by the agent's (own) reasons.

With the last statement we may agree. It is also true that motives and reasons are often called "causes of actions." There is no objection to this way of speaking as long as one does not let it obscure the conceptual differences between causes of events in nature and reasons for action. A minor objection to the position just described is that it is overly "rationalistic" if it assumes that *all* actions have a motive-explanation and that *no* action is therefore (completely) fortuitous.

This way of "reconciling" freedom and determinism is an interesting reflection of the prestige which deterministic ideas have enjoyed in our intellectual culture. By calling reasons for actions "causes," one can defend human freedom and at the same time pay lip-service to the deterministic world-view of classical natural science.

This defense of compatibilism leaves another problem unsolved, however. One could call it a problem of *congruence* or

---

[10] Schopenhauer's treatise on the Freedom of the Will (1841), still very much worth reading, may be regarded as the *locus classicus* for this position. Motives, on Schopenhauer's view, are causes and, as such, necessarily connected with the ensuing actions. Motivational causation he characterizes, interestingly, as "die durch das *Erkennen* hindurchgehende Kausalität." Schopenhauer quotes with approval Hume, who held "that the conjunction between motives and voluntary actions is as regular and uniform as that between cause and effect in any part of nature" (*Enquiry*, § VIII). A later writer in the same vein is Edward Westermarck in *The Origin and Development of the Moral Ideas*, I–II (London: Macmillan, 1906–1908).

[11] Cf. Westermarck, *Origin and Development*, vol. I, ch. XIII, for a good clarification of the distinction.

parallelism (cf. above, p. 112). Granting that reasons are causes, we seem to have two parallel but independent causal chains here. On one hand we have reasons causing actions, and on the other hand we have innervations and other neural processes causing muscular activity. The two chains converge in the physical aspect of the actions. How shall we understand the "congruence" or seeming "coincidence" that when I do a certain thing for one reason or other, the required physical aspect of my action makes its appearance under the influence of causes, perhaps acting from without my body, and in any case "external to my will"?

4. I open a lock — my arms and hands go through certain movements. Why do I open the lock? I want to fetch something from the locked cupboard. By *moving* my hands I *achieve* the unlocking of the cupboard. The *movements* of my hands *caused* the lock to open. What *made me* move my hands in a certain way? The fact that I wanted to unlock the cupboard or, perhaps, the fact that I wanted to fetch something from the cupboard. What *made my hands* move in a certain way? Some innervations of the muscles from the brain. What made those innervations take place (just) then? With this question the "problem of congruence" is raised — and the conceptual muddle begins.

I shall next introduce the notion of the *context* of an action.

Consider again the action of opening a lock. It has a beginning: I "embark" on the task, as we say, proceed to action. The action has a certain duration, lasts for some time during which my arms and hands go through certain movements. And it comes to an end: the lock opens. The things just mentioned constitute (describe) the context of the action.

Where in relation to this context shall we "locate" the innervations of the muscles? Obviously they do not begin when my arms and hands are already moving. They must be there when I embark on the task. They must belong *in* the context of my action. Perhaps they could be called the "physical aspect" of that somewhat "intangible" episode which I call "embarking on" an action. What is this?

My desire to fetch something from the cupboard may have already existed before I set myself to open the lock. The same holds for my want to open the lock. The origination of a want may be impossible to locate exactly in time. If the want was there before I embarked on the action (and its existence thus falls partly outside the "context" of the action), then proceeding to action consisted just in this, that some innervations put my arms and hands in motion. Embarking on the action *was* my want "becoming active," and this happened when the innervations put my arms and hands in motion. But are not these two things: proceeding to action and the innervations moving my hands really *the same*, only described in different ways? One description is in obscure "mentalistic" terms ("embarking on the action," "my want becoming active"), the other in, seemingly, clearer physical (neural) terms. I shall return to this question (below, p. 157ff).

5. Assume that the only explanation I could offer for the action is that I wanted to open the lock. Just this. Not that I wanted to find out whether I could open it or that I wanted to fetch something from the cupboard. It would be rather strange, just wanting that. It would be like saying "an irresistible desire overcame me." One could ask: Was my action free? There is not much *point*, it seems, in calling the action "free" if its context is, in the sense described, "self-contained."

Assume, however, that my action has a fuller explanation. I opened the lock because I wanted to fetch a bottle of wine from the cupboard. Why did I want this? Perhaps I was expecting guests for dinner. When the action is placed in this setting it seems artificial to speak of a (separate) "want" to open the lock.

The fuller explanation points beyond the context of the action. It points to the future — to an "end" being aimed at. It also points to the past — to a pre-existing want conditioned by an expectation. When set in this perspective, one would not hesitate to call my action of opening the lock "free." The context of the action is now embedded in a larger context of reasons and motivations.

This larger context is still "finite" in the sense that the chain of ever-remoter reasons has an end. I expected guests for dinner. This I obviously did for some reason. The normal reason would be that I had invited the people. But why? Perhaps because I had been invited to visit them before. By inviting them back I observe a rule of "good manners" in our society. And perhaps there are some other reasons too. But I shall probably not be able to advance in my explanation much beyond this point.

Although an explanation in terms of reasons may point far beyond the context of the action in time, the reasons must yet, all of them, be *present* in the context. The agent need not be aware ("thinking") of (all of) them when he proceeds to action. But they must be present in the sense that he subsequently can say, if challenged, that he *had them* then. He did not "invent" them afterwards, nor had he completely forgotten about them. He would have been able to state them when proceeding to action had he, for whatever reason, reflected on why he was doing what he was doing. But the borderline is often blurred between pre-existing reasons and a subsequent "rationalization" of an action.

When I set myself to act for some reasons, the motivation background present in the context of the action "activates me" — and the physical aspect of this activation is the "innervations" which make my muscles contract and relax and thus direct the bodily movements which constitute the physical aspect of my action. But how can the motivation background which moves *me*, the agent, to action have this power over the innervations which move my *muscles* if there is not something answering to this background on the physical side, i.e., in the brain or nervous system of the agent? The answer, presumably, is that the motivation background could *not* have this power unless it had some such "physical counterpart."

Assume that my action was the response to an order or was the answer to a question. I heard some noises which were an *order* to *me* to *do* a certain thing which I can do — and I proceeded to do it. The order was the reason why I acted. But the command had to be *understood* (not only "heard") in order to activate me. What is this? In order to understand an order I have to know the language in which it is issued and to hear it when it is issued. I also have to know the "meaning" of orders as reasons for action. All this must already be "embedded" in my past history, if the order is to move me to action. This again presupposes, as far as we know — and this is a matter of *empirical* (scientific) and *not* conceptual knowledge — that my nervous system has been duly prepared or "programmed" in the course of my development, i.e., growth and learning process. If, then, I receive an order and react to it, this means, in physical terms, that certain soundwaves affect my hearing (nerves), and the "message" is transported to the brain and effects a change in the neural patterns which eventually "releases" the innervations.

But must not *the brain* "understand" the "message" of the soundwaves in order to emit to the muscles the "message" of the innervations? Certainly — but it should be noted that speaking of "understanding" and of "messages" is here metaphorical talk. Its literal meaning is this: In order to come to understand commands (in the literal sense of "understand") I have to learn a language and to react to orders and other messages (in the literal sense of "message") — and this process involves a (physical) impact on my nervous system. My brain becomes programmed to certain reactions to stimuli. This does not mean that the same stimulus will invariably call forth the same reaction. The programming is to a complex of stimuli, and variations in this complex may cause variations in the reactions (responses). On the level of "mentalistic" talk this answers to the fact that there may exist several reasons for and several reasons against an action and also reasons which, although present, are not efficacious in relation to the action which eventually results from a "balancing" of the reasons for and against.

The upshot of our discussion of the parallelism between the reasons (motivation background) of an action and the innervations and neural patterns causally responsible for its physical aspect is thus as follows: To the *understanding* of the reasons (as reasons for or against an action) there answers a programmation of the neural apparatus, and to the *existence* of the reasons in the context of a certain action there answers a stimulation of this apparatus, and to the agent's proceeding to action there answer innervations of some muscles in the agent's body.

Two questions now arise: Do these correspondences amount to identities? And: What is the bearing of these correspondences on the problem of freedom?

6. I shall here introduce a technical term, *substrate*. And I shall say that the innervations under consideration are the substrate of the agent's setting himself to the action. Similarly, I shall call the muscular activity which constitutes the physical aspect of the action the substrate of the action. There is a reason why we cannot identify either the agent's setting himself to the action or the action itself with what I have called their "substrate." It is the following:

We could observe and accurately describe the muscular activity without knowing of which action it is the physical aspect. I see the agent's hands and arms go through certain movements manipulating a lock with a key. What is the agent doing? Unlocking the cupboard? This is one possibility. Or trying to see whether he can open it? (The trick may not be easy.) Or checking whether the key fits the lock? (There are many keys in the bunch, and the agent forgets from time to time which key matches which lock.) These are other possibilities. In order to know which of these actions the agent is performing, if any, we must know what he intended or "meant" by his behaviour. To find this out is usually not difficult. We do this by taking note of what preceded or what followed the performance or simply by asking the agent. But observations, however accurate, on his muscular activity alone cannot give us the answer (at most they may give rise to a surmise), because the substrate of an action does not stand in a one-to-one relation of correspondence to the action. And the same also holds good, of course, for the relation between the innervations and the agent's embarking on the action. Even if the innervations could be identified and described with great accuracy, *they* would not tell us which action the agent engages in.

But are not the muscular activity and the action, after all, the same reality, two different conceptualizations of what is here called "the substrate"? And the same with the innervations and the embarking on the action?

In some sense of "reality" they are the same. I shall call this their *robust* reality. The action is not anything over and above its physical aspect, if by "over and above" one understands some thing or some event in the physical world which one could identify as that which, when "added" to the muscular activity "makes up" the (whole) action. There is no such thing. And similarly for the innervations and their "equivalent" in actionistic terms.

So must we not say then that the action *is* identical with its physical aspect (muscular activity) and the agent's embarking on it identical with the innervations, i.e., with the neural cause of the muscular activity? The answer is No — for the reason already given, viz., that no description of the substrate would be sufficient to identify the action.

7. What causes the innervations to occur? Roughly speaking: Stimulations of a nervous system which has been "programmed" in the course of the lifetime of an individual (the agent) to respond in characteristic ways to stimuli of the kind under consideration. All this can, and should, be understood in strictly "physicalistic" terms — as soundwaves affecting the auditory nerves,

neurons firing, "engrammes" being implanted in the connections of nerve-fibres, etc., etc. The response is, in the last resort, the innervations which steer the muscles.

This is a sketchy description of what I propose to call the "substrate" of the motivation background present with an agent in the context of an action.

The overt *effect* of the reasons in moving the agent to action thus is the same as the overt *effect* of a physical stimulation of a "programmed" neural system, because either effect consists in that the agent's bodily organs go through certain movements. Does it follow that the reasons are identical with the physical stimuli? The answer is analogous to the answer we gave in order to clarify the distinction between action and muscular activity.

How does one establish that an agent has a certain reason for action, e.g., understands a command, believes that something is a means to an end, wants something and shuns something else? Partly by taking note of what he professes to understand, believe, want, etc., that is, by eliciting from him verbal responses to questions. But these are by no means the sole criteria — just as the reason the agent himself gives for an action need not settle the question why he acted. Further investigations about his past history or his subsequent behaviour may be called for, and the results of such investigations may override the verbal testimony of the agent. ("He cannot really believe what he says; he is too well educated for that, and his behaviour on other occasions speaks strongly against this.")

The existence of a reason is not anything which can be "pinned down" to the obtaining of a state of affairs or going on of a process at a certain time and place. It is a "global" fact of non-definite extension, a characteristic of the type of logical individual we call a "person."

The observations on behaviour (including verbal responses) on the basis of which we attribute to an agent a certain reason for action do not logically entail the existence of the reason. But they are not (only) signs or symptoms of something the existence of which could be established independently with "absolute certainty" on the basis of some "defining characteristics" *other* than those behavioural manifestations. This is why I shall call these latter "criteria" of (the existence of) the reasons.[12]

Neural states and processes do not, on the whole, serve as criteria of (the existence of) reasons. Perhaps they would be criteria *among others* if they were more manifest and accessible to inspection and better known than they are at present. But as things are, their "epistemological position" in relation to reasons is quite different. Suppose we had found out, by anatomic and physiological study of the nervous system, that in many cases there is a correlation between some kind of simple reason (e.g., being thirsty) for some simple type of action (e.g., drinking) and certain neural patterns and processes. We could then frame a *hypothesis* to the effect that this correlation holds also in unexamined cases, if not "without exception," at least with "high probability." This hypothesis could then be tested on further cases. Testing it — like making it — presupposes that we have already established on independent grounds the existence of the reason for action which is now being "matched" with a "corresponding" neural state. If the correspondence is well established, the neural state in question may be regarded as a reliable *sign* or *symptom* of the existence of the reason. As long as the correlation remains a scientific hypothesis, the neural state fulfils this rôle of a symptom. Only in the very unlikely case that the hypothesis became so well confirmed that we would be extremely reluctant to drop it when faced with seemingly contrary evidence could we conceivably use the neural state as a *criterion* of the agent's having a certain reason for action. And even then the criterion would only be one among many, and its

---

[12] The distinction between criteria and symptoms is familiar to every student of the later Wittgenstein. There is a vast literature commenting on the distinction, and many different interpretations have been offered of what Wittgenstein understood by the two terms. We need not add to the exegesis here.

usefulness in attributing to agents reasons for their actions would depend upon how well it contributed to our understanding of the agent as a person *and* to the agent's understanding of himself.

The above should suffice to make it clear why the *identification* of the existence of a reason with a correlated neural state is out of the question. And also that this is fully compatible with identifying the impact of the motivation background on the agent with the causing of the innervations which are responsible for the external aspect of the action (cf. above, p. 158).

About the nature of the causal mechanism not too much is known at present. More may be known in future. It cannot be regarded as certain that the correlation between a motivation background and its substrate is one-to-one in the sense that the presence of the same reasons will answer to the same neural states and processes causing the muscular activity in each context of the same action unless — which is always possible — one *postulates* the sameness and ascribes the difficulties in establishing it empirically to the play of (so far) unknown or unobserved factors.[13]

8. I hope I have succeeded in showing why it is no "accident" that when the reasons move the agent, the causes of muscular activity move his body "correspondingly." The idea of something accidental calling for an explanation is produced in us by the misleading picture of two parallel chains of independent and yet (in time) co-ordinated elements, viz., one chain of reasons and another one of causes, both chains converging in the action. From the point of view of their "substrate," i.e., their "robust," spatio-temporal reality, there is only *one* "chain."

If man from birth were endowed with a brain and a nervous system functioning in accordance with strict causal laws, and if this system never changed in the course of the development of the individual, then it would indeed be something of a "mystery" how

---

[13] Cf. Wittgenstein, *Zettel*, § 608 (Oxford: Basil Blackwell, 1967).

neurological causes could produce somatic effects (movements of the body) in "congruence" with our actions. But this idea of the brain as a system is not correct. When an infant grows up to be a member of a society, learns to speak and to do various things, to understand the meaning of challenges and institutions, and to participate in various practices, its nervous apparatus undergoes a simultaneous development partly of learning under the influence of external stimuli and partly of maturation of inborn capacities. The two processes go hand in hand and therefore the congruence between the mental and the bodily aspects of action is a *harmony* established in the course of the individual's life and necessary for its preservation over the span of time allotted to each of us.

That the solution we have given to the problem of congruence is not "materialistic" should be obvious. Less obvious is perhaps that it also involves no commitment to determinism.

Muscular activity is caused by innervations and innervations by stimulation of a "programmed" nervous system. Might not the stimulation in its turn be caused by events anterior to the context of the action, anterior even to the life-span (existence) of the agent, operating perhaps "from the dawn of creation"? So that then, by transitivity, the physical aspect of an action would be predetermined, in some cases at least, long before the action took place.

We have little reason to believe in such "rigid determinism" — and it is not even certain that it can be given a clear meaning (cf. below, p. 166). But let us not now question its possibility nor even its truth. Would this affect our view of the freedom of our actions?

9. Suppose that the action is one which we cannot connect in the understanding with any particular reason for doing it. We did it "for no particular reason." We cannot account for such "fortuitous" or "gratuitous" actions — except possibly by looking for causes of the movements which constitute their physical aspect (cf. above, p. 147). If we can find a cause, we should presumably

say that the action was not "free." We would treat it as a "reflex" rather than an action. If we cannot find a cause we should not know whether to call it "free" or not. Fortuitous actions, as we have observed before (above, p. 124f), have a peculiar relation to freedom just because they lack that which is the hallmark of free action, viz., to have been performed for some reason(s).

In order to have a clash or conflict between freedom and determinism we must imagine a case when there is both a reason-explanation and a causal explanation "at hand" which both are, somehow, of "the same thing." To imagine this, i.e., to describe correctly a case of conflict is not at all easy. As we shall see, it may not even be possible.

It is important here to see clearly the different nature of causal explanations and reason-explanations. A reason-explanation is of an action, a causal explanation of the physical (somatic) aspect of an action. A given display of muscular activity does not show "by itself" of which action it is the somatic aspect (cf. above, p. 157). Only in the case of some very simple actions such as, for example, the raising of an arm, may it seem pointless to separate the action from its physical aspect, for example the rising of an arm. What the causal (neurological) explanation can explain is the rising of the arm — and if the action performed was (just) the raising of the arm, one is tempted to say that one has a causal explanation of the action too. If, moreover, this action has no other explanation, was performed as we say for "no particular reason," then the causal explanation of its physical aspect is the sole explanation relating to this action which we have — and then, as we know, we may even be in doubt whether to call it an action at all. If, however, the action was, say, that I was reaching out to fetch a book from a shelf, the situation is different. There is no causal explanation of why I reach out for a book, although there may exist a causal explanation of why my arm reached, or failed to reach, the book I wanted (or had) to fetch. (This simple example should make us aware of the danger of using very "primitive" examples when discussing action. Arm-raising is one of the most favoured ones — but it is a *poor* example of an *action*.)

Since causal explanations and reason-explanations have different explananda there can be no "conflict" between the two types of explanation as such. But this does not yet show that there might not be a "conflict" between a reason-explanation of an *action* and a causal explanation of its *physical aspect*.

Assume next that we have these two explanations relating to the same action and assume further that the one makes reference to reasons which are present for the agent in the context of the action and the second to innervations caused by stimulations of the nervous system of the agent in that same context. Then there is no "conflict." *In the context of the action* there simply cannot *be* any "conflict" between the two explanations. On the contrary: we who share the "belief in science" of our century regard it as probable or even certain that if the action has a reason-explanation its somatic aspect has a causal explanation.

In order to give a causal explanation at all, it must have been established — using appropriate experimental techniques — that a certain stimulation of the nervous system *outside the context of any action* results in a certain type of muscular activity. (One should thus be able to "simulate" the somatic aspect also when no action of which it might be the somatic aspect takes place.)

For there to be a "conflict" between the two types of explanation we must now imagine a situation in which a certain action is performed and it is known that prior to the context of this action the agent's nervous system had been stimulated in a way which is bound by "causal necessity" to produce the somatic aspect of that same action. ("He had been secretly given an injection.") We must also imagine that the muscular activity occurs exactly when the agent performs the action. If it occurs before, the agent might say something like this: "Strange, I was just going to fetch a book from the shelf when my arm suddenly went up 'of itself' to the desired position." If it occurs again later, he might say:

"Strange, my arm did not rise at once when I was going to fetch the book, I had to wait a second."

If the agent himself knew of the operation of the cause he would also anticipate the display of muscular activity consequent upon it. ("Two minutes after the injection my arm will rise.") When the activity occurs he might use the opportunity for doing something for which those movements are required. ("When my arm rose, I snatched a book from the shelf." The snatching is then an action with a physical aspect of its own, e.g., closing my fingers round the book; the rising of the arm was just something which happened to me and "facilitated" the action.) But it is also possible, and perhaps more likely, that the agent, knowing what is going to happen to his body, will do nothing at all then.

Assume, however, that the agent does *not* know of the operation of the cause but that *we* know. The agent said he did something for a certain reason, and we say that the physical aspect of his action would have occurred even if he had not acted. Was his action free? Since he had a reason for his action it was what we call "free action." But suppose we did not only know of the operation of the cause, but that we had ourselves made it operative? ("We gave him an injection.") Shall we then say that the agent had been "manipulated"? This would not be right. His *body* had been manipulated. But since he happened to have reasons for doing an action the physical aspect of which consisted in the muscular activity which we had caused to happen, his *action* was not a result of manipulation. Only by influencing an agent's *reasons* can he be (genuinely) manipulated.

The sort of case we have been imagining is artificial and plays at most a marginal rôle in an agent's life. But more importantly: we have not succeeded yet in staging a genuine case of conflict between "freedom and determinism." Have we set ourselves an impossible task then? Let us make this final attempt:

Within the context of the action, could not the cause of the somatic aspect of the action in its turn have a cause operating from outside this context and thus, by transitivity, be itself the cause of the somatic aspect? Such an anterior cause would be a stimulus affecting the (programmed) neural state of an agent either from outside, say in the form of soundwaves, or from the inside, say in the form of cramps in the stomach. In the medium of the under-standing these affectations may appear as reasons for actions (to obey an order or to get something to eat) and in the medium of the nervous system they may release innervations guiding the somatic aspects of "corresponding" actions. Whether they will have this effect or not depends upon how the agent and his nervous system have been "programmed": the agent in the form of learn-ing and previous experience, his soma in the form of traces which learning and experience have left on it. Is this a "conflict between freedom and determinism"? I don't see how it could be called this. But the influences (stimulations) to which a person has been exposed in the course of his development (education and life ex-perience) and is currently exposed to in his social and physical situation determine to a great extent the reasons which he will have for actions and thereby also what he will do. This is a fact to which we have to acquiesce. It does not make a man unfree in the sense that he would not be acting for reasons. But it makes any man to some extent a "victim" of the circumstances of his life and sometimes also a victim of (genuine) manipulation by other agents. The circumstances of a man's life, and therewith the rea-sons he has for various actions, are *also*, however, to some extent of his own making (cf. above, p. 127).

10. Is every total somatic state rigidly determined causally by preceding somatic states? The answer is negative, since the somatic states are also causally dependent upon stimuli from outside the body. So the question is whether every total somatic state of the body is causally uniquely determined by preceding states and ex-ternal stimuli. But even with this obvious supplementation the *meaning* of the question is obscure.

What does the phrase "causally uniquely determined" mean? An answer could be: It means that from knowing the stimuli and the preceding states one could predict ("with certainty") the next state. But what is "the next" state? Do the successive total states form a discrete manifold then? And does a state depend causally only on the immediately preceding state, or also on patterns in the succession of (several) preceding states? We shall not even *try* to answer these questions. (Raising them will, however, give an idea of the conceptual obscurity surrounding our initial question.)

Predicting future states of the body on the basis of knowledge of stimuli and past states also presupposes knowledge of connecting *laws*. Such laws would, in the last resort, be generalizations from experience, i.e., from experiments and observations. Let us not question the possibility of knowledge of such laws.

In order to complete the deterministic picture we are drawing we have also to assume that all the stimulations which affect a body have a causal history which is strictly deterministic. We are thus forced to consider not only the total state of a body but much larger fragments of the total state of "the world" — and maybe not only fragments but the unbounded totality. In the end we may have to draw something like the suggestive picture of rigid determinism which Laplace impressed upon the scientific and philosophic imagination in an immortal passage in his *Essai philosophique sur les probabilités*.

But have not scientific developments in our century eroded and made obsolete the idea of rigid determinism in the physical world? At least at the microlevel there seem to exist "margins of indeterminacy" within which bodies can behave (move) freely. Neural states and processes are studied at the microlevel. One talks about "spontaneous activity" in the neural system. And some philosophers have hailed these developments in science as loopholes for "free will."

I hope that I have succeeded in showing that such pro's and con's of determinism are completely irrelevant to the philosophic problem of free action. Even the most rigid determinism in the physical world, which we could conceive as a logically consistent possibility, would not show that human beings are not free agents or that "free will" is only an epistemic illusion.

Determinism holds good, one could say, to the extent that it "works," i.e., we can successfully predict the future on the basis of past experience and hypothetically assumed laws of nature. Our success in this regard has been considerable. The search for causes and deterministic explanations has turned out to be immensely rewarding. Therefore it has been useful to entertain the idea of determinism as a heuristic maxim for guiding research. In many areas of science the idea is likely to continue to play its classic rôle. In other areas it may have to be modified ("relaxed") or it will be dropped as useless (cf. above, p. 150).

11. Have I wanted to say that the study of somatic states and processes is of no relevance to an account of actions in the terms of reasons? By no means have I wanted to say this.

Several of the basic "passions of the soul" have characteristic somatic accompaniments — other than the overt bodily expressions known of old to observers of human nature. This is true, for example, of anger and fear. They are "reflected" in measurable fluctuations in blood pressure or secretion of adrenalin. Observations on such changes may on occasion be relevant also to our understanding (explanation) of actions.

They might, for example, be used as a kind of "lie detector." An agent perhaps denies that he did something because he was afraid (of something he wished to escape) or because he was angry (with somebody and wanted to harm him). He may give an entirely different reason for his action. We doubt what he says — and a medical examination gives support to our suspicion.

Perhaps we can "force" the agent to admit that he was lying, hiding from *us* his real motives. But perhaps he had used a "noble" motive to hide an "ignoble" one not only from us but also from himself. He was "lying to himself" too (cf. above, p. 140).

What can our "lie detector" now achieve, if the agent himself was not even aware of fear or anger? Great caution is needed when trying to decide such cases. Perhaps the wise thing is to suspend judgement. But maybe we can make the agent realize that there was something in the situation that he actually feared or that actually had angered him — although he says he did not "feel" fear or anger then. This may make him more watchful (reflective) of his subsequent conduct. In this way he may arrive at a changed self-understanding in the light of which he will also view some of his past actions differently.

12. Do animals act?

We do not easily say that they do. To say that an animal "performed" this or that action — or omitted to perform one — even sounds a bit comical or ludicrous. It sounds like a "personification" of the animal — such as is common in fables and tales. But animals, "really," are not persons. (Some, however, can be "characters" or even "personalities.")

Animals, of course, *do* a lot of things. But this holds also of many inanimate objects; our language is permeated by "actionistic" ways of talking about things that ("passively") take place.

Yet animal behaviour also has many features in common with human action. Animals *learn* to do various things — which they then do on "appropriate" occasions. When thirsty they exhibit "water-seeking behaviour," when hungry they "go for food," to use the jargon of psychologists. How like or unlike human hunger and thirst is animal hunger and thirst? This is a philosophically interesting question — but I shall not go into this topic here.

Aiming, intending, can certainly be attributed to animals. Whether we should say that animals "have" aims and intentions is less certain. Animals make choices. They may, perhaps, even be "torn between alternatives," like Buridan's famous ass.

Animals are free when they are not (physically) prevented or restrained from doing what otherwise they would do. But are their doings free in the sense human actions are? In what sense then are human actions free? Free action is action for reasons, I have said. (And action, essentially, is behaviour for reasons; the adjective "free" in "free actions" is redundant except when it means absence of "compelling reasons.") That animals do not act is connected with the fact that they do not possess the self-reflective capacity which "having reasons for actions" is. And this again is connected with the limited linguistic capacities of animals.

Since animals do not act for reasons, *why* do they behave as they do? Descartes thought that animals were machines, automata. If this means that animal action, to the extent that it can be explained at all, must be explained as *reactions to* (inner and outer) *stimuli*, I think Descartes was right. The other type of explanation of behaviour, viz., in terms of reasons for action, simply does not *apply* to animals.

Human behaviour too — including the physical aspects of actions — may be studied as reactions to (inner and outer) stimuli. Man is no less a machine than animals are. Rather one should say that he is "more" of a machine because his machinery is more complex, more developed. It is not by being exempted from the bondage of natural law that man is a free agent. He is this because we can understand him in a way, viz., as a person, in which we — or most of us at least — cannot understand the rest of creation.

The Future of the Atlantic Alliance

HELMUT SCHMIDT

THE TANNER LECTURES ON HUMAN VALUES

Delivered at
The University of Utah

April 4, 1984

HELMUT SCHMIDT, former Chancellor of West Germany from 1974 to 1982, is a native of Hamburg, where he was educated in political and economic science and took a degree in economics in 1948. As a Social Democrat, he came to his chancellorship having studied the workings of German economic policy firsthand as Joint Minister of Economics and Finance and as Finance Minister in earlier governments. While in office, he pushed a treaty for the normalization of relations between West Germany and Czechoslovakia and the nullification of the Munich Pact of 1938, and the stabilization of international relations and détente continue to be his major concerns. Among Mr. Schmidt's publications are *Defense or Retaliation: A German View*, and *The Balance of Power: Germany's Peace Policy and the Superpowers*. In 1972 he received the U.S. Medal for Distinguished Service.

President Peterson, Professor Dick, Ladies and Gentlemen,
thank you very much for your kind words of introduction and be
assured that at the age of sixty-five I won't blush about your flatter-
ing remarks.

I do intend tonight to speak first about the evolution of the
grand strategy of our alliance over the last thirty-five years; sec-
ond, I will look briefly at the economic deficiencies of our alliance;
and third, I will make some remarks about the Soviet Union and
our relationship with that country.

I would also like to say a few words about the Europeans and
their difficulties at the present time. Within this context I will dis-
cuss some principles of military strategy and, finally, I would like
to say a few more words about leadership within an alliance of
sovereign states.

Regarding the evolution of the grand strategy of our alliance,
it seems to me that so far we have witnessed three stages, and
today we are in the middle of a discussion about the fourth stage.
Henry Kissinger's article in *Time* magazine in early March of
1984 was a contribution to that fourth stage. As of today we are
still scrabbling and babbling and nobody really has a clear-cut
view, but this is not uncommon. It sometimes has taken a couple
of years for the Alliance jointly to come to new insights.

The first phase of our grand strategy was a rather short one.
It was essentially defined by the United States alone, due to the
situation of that time. I am talking about the years immediately
after the war, when the United States presented to the Soviet
Union the Baruch Plan, aimed at joint and total renunciation of
nuclear weapons, and the Marshall Plan, which aimed at the joint
reconstruction of the European countries devastated by the war.

The Soviet Union rejected both offers, much to their disadvantage. They did not participate in the Marshall Plan, which was carried out anyway. The Baruch Plan could not enter into force without Soviet participation. Instead, Stalin consolidated Russian rule over the states and peoples of Eastern Europe. He threatened Berlin, the big city, the old German capital in the center of Europe, and he laid the foundations of Russian nuclear missile and satellite armaments. Thereby he did provoke and contribute to the beginning of the second phase of the Western grand strategy very soon after the war.

The second phase was characterized by the foundation of the Atlantic Alliance. It was characterized not so much by the then American foreign secretary's terminology (I am referring to John Foster Dulles and his "roll back" strategy) but rather by George Kennan's catchword "containment." Containment was a concept that he developed, if I am not mistaken, as early as 1947 — at that time not under his own name but as the famous "Mr. X" in an article in *Foreign Affairs* in July of 1947.

Containment of the Russians was more or less the essence of the second phase of Western grand strategy. It was the goal of containment which induced John Foster Dulles to create his anti-Soviet system of alliances all over the globe. Some of the alliances created at that time have since been dissolved. This period also embraced a specific doctrine of military strategy, mainly the deterring threat of what was then called "massive (nuclear) retaliation," or, so to speak, massive nuclear punishment if the Soviets ever undertook to trespass the boundaries. I won't go into the details of that period. I would just like to say that President Kennedy's management of the Cuban missile crisis in 1962 appears, in retrospect, as the culminating point of that period as well as the end of the second phase of massive nuclear retaliation.

The third phase of the third stage of the grand strategy had started a bit earlier than 1962. I would like to recall the book of a great American army general, Maxwell D. Taylor, that was published in 1959 under the title *The Uncertain Trumpet*. Here a military man analyzed the situation, namely what will happen if we do let loose the big nuclear stick, and he was quite convinced that it was rather unlikely that Americans would ever do it.

In the beginning of the 1960s then, let us say more concretely in 1962, the United States drew two important conclusions from a debate in which Maxwell Taylor and others, including the Europeans and the British, had already been engaged for a couple of years. Number one, America abandoned the military strategy of massive nuclear retaliation in favour of a new military strategy of what later was called flexible response. Incidentally, this replacement of one military strategy with another for fifteen years, one-and-a-half decades, has been the only unilateral action of the United States within the Alliance. It was initiated by the then defense secretary Robert S. McNamara at a meeting of allied defense ministers in Athens in 1962, but it took the European allies five more years, until the end of 1967, to agree on the strategy of flexible response.

The second conclusion drawn by the U.S. from the nuclear strategic stalemate with the Russians was of much greater importance. It was a conclusion in the field of grand strategy of which military strategy is just one component (not necessarily the most important component in all circumstances), the consequence of which was an expansion of U.S. cooperation with the Soviet Union into new fields, with the full approval and active participation of America's European and Canadian allies.

So in 1967, after some preparation the Alliance jointly agreed on the dual grand strategy and approach that retained its validity until the Carter Administration, namely, military deterrence through the capability of flexible military defense, on the one hand, and cooperation with the Soviet Union in the field of arms control and arms limitation on the other. It was basically with full support of the allies, North American and European, that in accordance with this double-track grand strategy approach towards the Soviet Union, the test ban treaty was concluded with the Soviets. Then came the treaty on the non-proliferation of nuclear weapons in the late sixties; the Salt I agreement between President Nixon and General Secretary Brezhnev; the German treaties with Moscow, Warsaw, East Berlin, and Prague; the Four-Power Agreement on Berlin; later in 1975 the Final Act of Helsinki; then shortly after that the German–Polish agreements; and last, Salt II under President Carter. It is indicative that Salt II was negotiated and agreed upon but never ratified in this country because of strong opposition within the United States. But the agreement is still being honored not just by one but by both sides.

This third phase of the grand strategy which started gradually in the mid-sixties and lasted until the beginning of the second half of the seventies, from my point of view — let me say from a general political point of view — has come to be the most fruitful so far. Rather than thinking in categories of punishment or retaliation we began thinking in terms of an equilibrium between the West and the East. We began to understand that the West and the East had to accept their responsibility to preserve stability in the interest of peace. This understanding was underlined in 1967, when the Alliance adopted the so-called Harmel Report, actually a report of all the fifteen nations, written under the chairmanship of Belgian Foreign Secretary Pierre Harmel. (By the way, this Harmel Report was the document through which the word détente was incorporated into official NATO language. For some in America it has since become a dirty word. I deplore this, but I understand that it is a fact of life that right now it is not advisable to use the word if you don't wish to be disliked in this country more than necessary.)

During the thirty-five years since the beginning of the Alliance it has withstood a number of strategic crises in an astonishing way. There was the Cuban missile crisis. There was the crisis created by the abrupt departure of France from the NATO military integration (with France remaining a member of the Alliance, however).

There was the catharsis of the Vietnam war and the domestic post-Vietnam political crisis in your country, accentuated by Watergate — which did not have any major effect on the cohesion between North America and Europe or on the cohesion and overall strategy of the Alliance as a whole.

It is true that President Nixon struck the Europeans as morally dubious but at the same time as a completely acceptable strategic leader of the Alliance. And many of you may be astonished that his name is being used in political circles in Europe nowadays with some respect as regards his strategic performance. President Gerald Ford, who, in European eyes, was and still is considerably underestimated in his own country, did continue Nixon's grand strategy.

By the way, Jerry Ford never tried to dictate unilateral American decisions to the European allies. As a leading representative of the Alliance, Ford was fully accepted in Europe. Let me tell you a little story about Jerry Ford. We met here last fall in Vail, Colorado. There was the landlord of course, and his wife, there was Henry Kissinger, there was former French president Valéry Giscard d'Estaing, there was Jim Callaghan, former prime minister of Britain, and then there was myself. We had a nice discussion about world affairs. We were not totally satisfied about the situation, and at the end of the night Jerry Ford summed it all up by saying: "Well, gentlemen, I guess we all can agree that the world was much better off in our time."

It was first in the Carter era that, through some rather drastic moves without previous consultation with other allies, the Alliance was strained. And it happened in two areas at the same time. Against European advice, the Americans threw overboard the Ford-Kissinger Salt II approach, and we Europeans were also emphatically called upon to increase our budgetary deficit spending in order to get the world's economy going. We were asked to take inflationist measures. Both Paris and Bonn reacted sourly, of course. We didn't do it. We wanted to maintain our one-digit inflation rates as President Peterson [of the University of Utah] hinted at earlier on, and we did not have the feeling that America could act as a leader in the economic field every time.

President Reagan inherited a delicate intra-Alliance situation. He tried to restore the American position of leadership by drastic unilateral action, not necessarily to the satisfaction of his allies. He could count on firm domestic political support, but he did not, in the first instance, find much agreement on the part of the allies.

So over the last seven years, the consensus on the common grand strategy has been lost. The European allies were dismayed and concerned about the two-year-long neglect of arms limitation negotiations and by the apparent striving for American military superiority rather than equilibrium.

And all this, and I am coming to my second subject rather soon, had a bearing also on the economic situation of the European countries. "Supply-side" economics is in fact a rebirth of Keynesian deficit spending, the one exception being that Keynes thought of printing the money and nowadays it is being borrowed. The enormous budgetary deficits in America have increased the economic difficulties of the European partners, and this deficit spending policy was totally unexpected in Europe. The high interest rates which result from the deficit are the highest real interest rates the world has seen since the birth of Christ. In the meantime they have let the world's richest country, the richest society, the richest economy, become the world's greatest net importer of credit and capital. The export of inflation from Europe to North America and the increase in real interest rates, really meaning the difference between nominal interest rates and inflationary rates, have occurred at the expense of real investment in productive capital all over the world and therefore at the expense of employment. And they also have occurred at the expense of the non-oil-exporting developing countries which find themselves in a position of being unable to cover the costs of their debts. They will never pay back the principle, this is assured, for they even have enormous difficulty in paying the interest because the rates have gone up and up and up for them over the last couple of years. On the other hand, this enormous capital influx into the United States has resulted in very high exchange rates for the dollar — quite nice for the Europeans because it's easier to sell European-manufactured goods in the United States and other dollar areas, and not so nice for your industry because sometimes you can't even compete with imported European and Japanese goods in your own markets, and sometimes you certainly cannot compete with Japanese and European goods in other markets due to the high exchange rate of the dollar.

So all this has led to tendencies toward protection, protectionism, and subsidization. Protectionist measures on this side of the Atlantic of course provoke protectionist measures on the other side of the Atlantic or the Pacific. I would say that international commerce has deteriorated to the point that less than one half of the world's trade is free, the greater half suffering from the impact of either protective measures or subsidization. And this is true for products from steel to grain.

At the same time, we have seen an enormous weakening of the global monetary structure. The total effect plus the prospect for the future has shaken every government in Europe. No government in Europe has been able to maintain its position. All of them have been toppled due to the fact that the public normally hold their government responsible if the economy is not really doing well, and even Margaret Thatcher, shortly after her overwhelming election victory, has come under heavy domestic pressure; the British public opinion polls show that if there were a new election tomorrow she might lose. Of course, the United States is totally unconscious of the effects of the nation's economic behaviour on the rest of the Alliance. And this innocent lack of awareness was reflected in the economic cover story of the same issue of *Time* magazine which printed the Kissinger article that I mentioned earlier on. The story was eight pages of analysis and prognosis of the bad effects of the United States' super deficit, but there was not a single word concerning the effects in the Third World, in the developing world, in Europe, or elsewhere.

I will soon leave the economic area, but I would like to state before doing so that a grand strategy must finally include once more the global economic conduct of all its partners, as was the case during the seventies — or at least that we try as we did in seven or eight economic summits, one after the other starting in 1975, to coordinate our economic and financial monetary policies. By the way, a provision asking for economic cooperation existed from the beginning in the North-Atlantic Pact. It still stands. Grand strategy of course needs a foundation of not only military but also political and economic solidarity among allies, although we will also be competitors in the foreseeable future. But it also requires some limitation and some curbing of competition and self-interest among allies, although competition and self-interest remain unavoidable in principle.

Let me now come to the Soviet Union and our relationship with her. The new grand strategy which might evolve over the next few years must make it clear that the effort is not towards superiority over the Soviet Union but towards equilibrium with her. And to this goal armament policy and military posture have to be subordinate. But above all, the diplomacy of arms limitation has to serve the goal of balance. There have been some errors in arms limitation and détente in the past. For instance, there was a Western error regarding détente. When we accept an approximate military balance in Europe, we must know that thereby neither the Middle East nor Central America nor Africa nor Afghanistan nor Cambodia, and so on, is ensured against advancing Soviet influence. It was always clear, to me at least, that the SALT treaty could not rescue Vietnam or Cambodia or Afghanistan. And whoever makes détente or arms limitation policy responsible for these successes of Russian expansionism because arms control was limited to so-called strategic weapons, and détente was politically limited to Europe only — whoever makes arms control responsible for expansionist successes of the Soviet Union only shows that he had illusions when these treaties were concluded. The fact is, rather, that it remains essential for America to assume the role of global counterforce. It is primarily in this worldwide context and through this role that the qualitative difference between Europe and the United States of America remains inevitable and necessary. For at this level, the Europeans cannot successfully operate alone or autonomously, whereas the United States can.

Now, in turn, there are two Russian errors concerning détente. Moscow has fully observed all treaties with the West and still is holding to them. In the non-treaty regions, however, the Politburo has expanded its power without respect for the interests of other states and nations. That goes for the exorbitant arming with SS-20 rockets — nowadays each of the rockets has three warheads and all together they are nearing a thousand warheads — which the West did not try to prevent through negotiations concerning strategic arms limitation agreements, and which today threatens all of Europe, the Mediterranean Coasts, including parts of Africa, the entire Middle East, and almost all of Asia, including the People's Republic of China and Japan. And this applies as well to the constant and persistent political and military extension of the Soviet spheres of influence on all the continents but Europe and Australia. This Russian expansionism, to be sure, was not forbidden by the ratified treaties that are mentioned earlier on, although, of course, it is a considerable infringement of international law and in many cases of the United Nations Charter. But the central point of my argument is that for years the Politburo assessed your reaction and the world's reaction all wrong. The Soviet Union, uninvited, provoked a young and optimistic nation, provoked you, to a great new effort and did thereby touch off a new argument. Due to that argument race, the Russians and the other peoples of the Soviet Union and the Comecon now have to undergo economic suffering as part of the consequences of this new arms race.

Let me say a few words about the Russians: I'm always struck by the fact that in this country the knowledge of the Russians does not go very deep and does not go very far back into history. Mostly, you only go back some forty years to Stalin, who has been called "Uncle Joe" in this country. What an evolution of language, by the way, from "Uncle Joe" to the "Empire of evil." But what you do not see is that before Stalin there were the tsars for more than four hundred years. And Stalin's deeds did not differ very much from what the tsars did. Whether Catherine the Great or Peter the Great or Ivan the Terrible or Ivan the Third or Ivan the First, they all were gatherers of Russian soil, as one of the titles the tsars bore indicates. What was really intended was to conquer other people's soil and afterwards russify the inhabitants. And so they did. Time and again they tried to get to the West, and time and again they conquered and subdued Poland and the other Baltic nations, the Lithuanians, the Estonians, the Latvians, sometimes the Finns, and time and again they tried to possess everything from the Balkans to Istanbul, then Constantinople. They enlarged their empire to the south and to Central Asia.

This is not Russia's first attempt to conquer Afghanistan; they tried to do it in the nineteenth century. They took away parts of what was then imperial China. They stretched out over the whole range of Siberia and russified it. You have four time zones in the United States; they have ten, it is such a large country. They even went over the Bering Strait to Alaska, which you bought from them just in time. Russia has always been an expansionist power.

And remember, it is the only imperialism, the only expansionism in history that never has been crushed. They have been defeated several times, but Russian expansionism never has been crushed. Spanish and Portuguese imperialism were worn out centuries ago. The French and British empires were given up after World War II. Japan's and Hitler's and Mussolini's imperialism were crushed in World War II. The Russians are the only ones left. And this has nothing to do with Communism or Marxism. It's

Russia, and it is a grave mistake to believe that all their behaviour is dictated by Marxism or Leninism. I would say their behaviour is three-fourths Russian and maybe 25 percent Communist.

One needs to understand Russian history in order to understand the motivations of the Russians. Except for a very small, thin upper rank of the nobility, they have never seen human rights. They have suffered for five centuries. They are great sufferers. Sometimes they even have a passion for suffering. You can understand this if you read their great novelists of the nineteenth century, the Pushkins and the Dostoevskis, the Tolstois, and the rest. They suffered under Stalin. They did not like Stalin, but nevertheless they fought for their country. They are great patriots; they have always been patriots despite all their suffering. Under Stalin they lost twenty million lives in the war against Hitler, and still they fought on and won the war in the end — together with you and your help as allies.

They will also suffer in the future, if necessary. If somebody on this side of the Atlantic dreamed of an arms race which would economically strangle the Russians, he or she would be wrong. They can be told by their Politburo that this is just another attempt at conquering them, at winning a victory over their country and that they must resist the attempt, and therefore they must tighten their belts even more, and they will, although grudgingly, do so, just do it, and the military might then get not only 12 or 13 percent of the GNP but maybe 15 or 16 percent. It's a deep misunderstanding of the Russian people to believe that you can strangle them economically or otherwise.

As an example, in my city of Hamburg, where I was born and raised, and which I have represented in Parliament for thirty-one years, my forbears were trading with the Russians in Novgorod 500 and maybe even 600 years ago. It was part of our life; they are so close by. We live by trading. And of course not only their literature — I mentioned some novelists of world importance — but also their music has become part of our culture: Tchaikowsky,

Prokofiev, and others. Look where Isaac Stern was born or where the parents of Leonard Bernstein came from. So in part they belong to Europe and in part they are a menace to Europe.

And we have always felt that one needs to contain them, which is necessary as a matter pertaining to military capabilities, not just diplomacy; but on the other hand, we also have felt that by geopolitical fate we are close to each other and that one should try and live in as good a neighbourhood as possible. And, of course, in the last thirty-five or forty years the European neighbourhood has been much, much closer to you, and this is understandable. We all have, I do not know how many, grandparents in common. It is one of the reasons why we understand each other so well, the Europeans and the Americans, the North Americans, and why we have the feeling of belonging to each other.

But, of course, we do also differ in many cases. The United States is such a big country and such a huge nation that you often are tempted to be satisfied to settle your own business within your own borders and not really look to the rest of the world. Also, you are a young and, therefore, an optimistic nation. Never in the two centuries of your history have you been defeated by foreign armies on your own soil. The Europeans, except the British, have been defeated by foreign armies time and again.

The Europeans have a long history, at least ten centuries — in the case of the Greeks and the Italians even twenty-five centuries — and we have also fought wars against each other time and again. Despite our belonging to the same European Christian culture, our languages have been differentiated from each other for much more than a thousand years — in some cases for 'a million years. Altogether, we Europeans are rather old nations and, therefore, we are much more sceptical than you Americans. The scepticism stems from long historical experience. Most Europeans look with some envy upon your great vitality. At least I do.

This is my sixtieth or sixty-first visit to the United States within the last thirty-four years, and this number shows, I hope, how important a European political leader evaluates America. But on the other hand, I have met quite a few of your countrymen who have made their first trip to the old continent only after receiving nomination as presidential candidates or even after having been elected President. So, what I am trying to say is that your political leaders tend to underestimate European interests as well as European historical experience. Let me give you just three examples:

1. We Europeans have come to understand that continuously maintaining an equilibrium of power *vis à vis* the Soviet Union is necessary, although it is not in itself a sufficient precondition for maintaining peace. You Americans, on the other hand, tend to downplay such thinking as being pragmatic. Pragmatism is sometimes not so nice a word in America, one viewed as being close to immoral, whereas you idealistically believe in rather high goals for foreign policies.

2. As I said, we Europeans live close to the Russians. We know that their expansionism has not changed much since the communists came to rule if compared with the four prior centuries. But you do not really try to understand the Russians and, therefore, many of your strategic goals are not really to the point because your knowledge of the psychology of the other side — namely an enormous security complex plus an inferiority complex — is simply not good enough.

3. We Europeans try to stick to one and the same basic line of policy and grand strategy, whether we change our governments once a year like Italy, or whether we change our Presidents only once in seven years like France. DeGaulle, Pompidou, Giscard, Mitterrand have not really changed their political strategy. Or whether you have rather frequent, more frequent changes, as in Britain: Ted Heath, Wilson, Callaghan, Thatcher. Or in Germany: Willy

Brandt, myself, Helmut Kohl right now. It would be very difficult for an American commentator or analyst to discover whether there are any important changes in the foreign policies of these European countries. Bipartisan foreign policies are not declared, but in fact are. (The Europeans, by the way, would be very happy if your great country would find its way back to a bipartisan policy; this would save us from the necessity of adapting ourselves to changing foreign policies every four years, sometimes even more often.)

Now the Europeans are in bad shape. The European economic community is politically sick because all its member countries are economically sick. The European allies as a group were not up to the dual challenge of, on the one hand, the economic turbulence since the second oil price explosion in 1979 to 80, plus, on the other hand, the abandonment of continuity in American foreign policy. European governments have turned out to be overburdened, so it is understandable to me that impatience and bitterness about Europe is proliferating in your country.

I totally agree with John Kennedy's great vision of the two pillars on which the Atlantic community should rest, the North American pillar and the European Community. But France has only one foot in the Atlantic Alliance, and Great Britain has only one foot in the European Community. My country, of course, is fully within both of these international communities, but my country obviously suffers from the awareness that in a crush Germany would be reduced to the role of a battlefield and suffers as well from the partition, from the division of the German nation.

That, by the way, is one of the reasons why the Germans are shocked more than other Europeans by the definite worsening of the East–West climate.

The Germans had erroneously taken détente as a sure thing forever. And many of the French and quite a few Americans,

today, misunderstand the German trauma as pacifism or as na-
tionalism. The French, for instance, had taken for granted the
role of the Federal Republic as a buffer, as a glacis or as an advance combat post. And so they have come to the illusion that the
Germans are the only nation in Europe to have really given up
their national identity. No, they have not.

The Europeans are a group you Americans would like to regard as a single ally. Even Henry Kissinger talks of "the Europeans" in his quoted article.

One rather often hears in your country, "why don't you Europeans just form a United States of Europe, as we have done in
America?" Some of the reasons we do not have something to do
with the fact of more than a thousand years' history of controversy
and antagonism, and you tend mostly to overlook the several
thousand years of speech barriers in Europe. You must also not
overlook the differing categories of political status. There are
nuclear states like France and Britain and non-nuclear states like
the rest. Some have veto powers as United Nations members, like
France and Britain again, and the rest are normal United Nations
members. With regard to Berlin, there are guarantee powers and
receivers of guarantees and so on. I think that most Americans are
not aware of these differentiations in Europe, and this is why you
tend toward an understandable impatience with, and in some cases
even contempt for, Europe. But be sure that, the other way around,
people in Europe tend to a non-understanding rejection of America's blowing both hot and cold.

To end this discussion before getting on to military strategy,
let me mention that the Kissinger article I have cited also says that
if one country dominates the alliance in all essential matters, as
you do, being big and powerful, then there remains for the dependent members hardly a stimulus for serious efforts at political
coordination. Well, I let this stand as it stands, but I would like to
add that dependency does corrupt — and it corrupts not only the
dependent partners but also the oversized partner who is making

decisions almost single-handedly. Now we ought on both sides of the Atlantic to make an effort to get back to joint decision-making in order not to let ourselves be corrupted because of being too dependent or because of being too big.

Now a word on military strategy. I think it is a fact that most of the European governments rely too much on American nuclear weapons and that the conventional defenses are, to some degree, being neglected by some European countries. And I think it is also a fact that both the United States and the Europeans at present are placing an unsuitably high value on nuclear deterrence. The so-called flexible response which I mentioned earlier on is no longer really flexible. In case of a defense operation it would be flexible only for a very short period, days rather than weeks. It has in fact become a military strategy of inflexible response because, due to the lack of conventional forces, the situation would very soon escalate into the nuclear field, and that means the destruction of Central Europe. That is why within the framework of a newly formulated grand strategy of the Alliance a reform of the military component is also necessary. I am not arguing for abstention from nuclear weapons, but I am arguing in favour of a better conventional balance. It is not necessary to be able to place one West German soldier in the field for every Soviet soldier. The defender can make do with certain numerical inferiority, but an improved military equilibrium does require improved military outfitting of the manpower reserves and requires secondarily the creation of reserves of British military personnel. And it requires in the third place a strengthening of the conventionally committable German air force and more conventional ammunition for the German army.

Let me tackle a few principles of military strategy. I have devoted part of my time to that over the last twenty-five years and to grand strategy as well. I have written books and I have been the defense secretary of my country, which under the German constitution also means the Supreme Commander.

Let me outline a few principles of military strategy from experience. I believe that the instruments and methods of implementation of one's military strategy must vary due to circumstances, due to technological progress or the state of the art, and so on. But the principles, I guess, remain the same. And a shorthand description, very superficially articulated, would contain six principles:

1. The *principle of deterrence*. To deter any possible or potential adversary from aggression by showing him that you are able to inflict damage upon him is not an invention of the last twenty-five years. The principle of deterrence has existed throughout history, which, at the same time, means that it hasn't always worked well.

2. Make the potential adversary understand, that we will in fact have the means and the goods to execute what we threaten to do. Never threaten something which we are not prepared to do in the event. That is the worst thing one can do. So I call this second point the *principle of credibility*.

3. You have to reckon with the possibility that deterrence could fail, and then you would actually have to defend your territory against violations whether they are on land or at sea or from the air or from space. You need the means to do so. This I call the *principle of adequacy* of defense.

4. And this then very quickly leads to the fourth principle, namely the *principle of continuous reevaluation* of what is adequate.

5. In the first place, of course, not only in the diplomatic but also in the military field, one has to put oneself in the shoes of the adversary, to try to understand the situation from his point of view, from his point of interest. Try to understand his interest, his posture, his plans, and to evaluate them. Do not threaten him into irrational behaviour; don't scare

him, that is, into an irrational arms race, but try to convince him that he can also feel secure. Without going into any further detail I would call this the *principle of equilibrium* or balance of power.

By the way, as a German living just some twenty miles from the iron curtain, it would take me just three quarters of an hour to meet the first Russian tank division. It would take them thirty-five minutes to get to my place. Well, it's easy to laugh about this if you live in Salt Lake City. In our situation we have long since understood that there is no such thing as total security for one side only. It is a utopian concept between two so powerful adversaries as are the Soviet Union and their alliance on the one side and our alliance on the other. It should be understood that ultimate security for one side would mean ultimate insecurity for the other, and to some degree they ought to understand their roles as being partners in security. This is some of the reasoning in depth behind the principle of equilibrium and balance of power.

6. The sixth principle has come more into the open only in the last couple of years, and that is the *principle of acceptability* of one's own strategy. Let me deal with that. Of course, the first five principles do raise questions, such as what is credible, what will be credible tomorrow, what is adequate today, what will it be tomorrow, where do we have equilibrium, and how do we stabilize it. But, obviously, the credibility of some of our former postures and plans suffers nowadays from growing deficits in our own public opinion. In all our parliaments, in the United States Senate, in all our churches and universities, whether in North America or Europe, in many, many places throughout the Western community, there are growing deficits regarding the acceptance of our own strategy.

I will mention a few examples that can make this deficit clear. For instance, the various freeze proposals coming out of America: it's an American invention, the no-early-first-use proposal regarding nuclear weapons, or the more radical or fundamental no-first-use proposal, or the various concepts invoked during the ongoing debate on rapid deployment forces or the missiles; or the debate going on about the Pershing-2 in Europe and the ground-launched cruise missiles in Europe. Obviously, we are to a much higher degree than ever before in some trouble with our credibility at home over the acceptability of our military postures and plans. And if we are not successful in convincing our public, then public opinion might lead to a situation wherein parliaments might not give us adequate laws and adequate means.

Look, for example, to what religious leaders in your country have had to say about all these questions. I have read it with great interest. Those in my country and in others have taken up the issue as well. Political leaders are being seriously questioned about our morality, that is, in connection with our military plans. Well, I think in general for a democratic society this is a necessary debate, and at least it is an unavoidable debate. It is a serious task to provide the answers to that debate and to provide the answers in due course of time and not only from hindsight.

If one fails to provide the answers, our credibility also as far as deterrence is concerned *vis-à-vis* the adversary will suffer dangerously. This is a very important insight. If we do fail to convince our own public, our own parliaments, how can we hope to convince the Soviet Union? If our credibility suffers in the eyes of our own public, then the credibility or strategy of course will also suffer, as will the evaluations of those twelve or thirteen leaders in the Kremlin.

So, obviously, the principle of acceptability of our military strategy is of growing importance. One cannot impose a military strategy on one's own forces in an open society that has not been accepted at least by the majority of one's society. Those times when rulers could do so are over, and no strategy will be accepted tomorrow and the day after which projects the probability of destroying what one wishes to defend.

It's easy to say this in an academic forum; it's easy to say this in America, but it has a much deeper meaning in Germany. It has the meaning that no strategy will in the long run — and the long run is not that long — be accepted in my country that threatens to destroy my country. We wish to defend our countries. I have said that Germany is about the size of Utah, in terms of territory, but there are sixty million people, six or seven armies, and on top of those armies we have five thousand nuclear weapons on our soil already. And the people living in the neighbourhood of these weapons think, very naïvely, but very correctly, that they are nice little targets for Russian nuclear rockets. They are targets, and a few more are being stationed right now and will be stationed during the next two years.

Think of all this happening on the soil of Utah, and you will understand why there is a peace movement in my country. I am not a member of it, I have been fighting it, but I wish you to have some understanding for the concern and anxiety of some of my people and countrymen. It's a densely populated area, very close to the Russians, with a dense population of nuclear weapons as well. I dare to prophesy that the idea of first use of nuclear weapons by ourselves against merely conventional violations from their side will in the course of the later eighties be evaluated more and more as being inadequate and more and more as being unacceptable. I think this is foreseeable. We had better prepare for a change in our military posture.

I was talking about manpower and manpower reserves. I was Secretary of Defense at the time when the United States abandoned the draft in national service in order to calm down campus unrest in the very early seventies. We decided to maintain it. It was not easy to explain to the German public that the Americans thought they could defend themselves without the draft while we couldn't, while we needed to maintain it. I am still sticking to that decision, as do the French and others on continental Europe, because I still believe that in order to defend one's country what one needs in the first place is men in uniform, soldiers. That is the first priority. And secondly one needs motivation in these men and thirdly one needs education in military skill and military training and personal capabilities in one's soldiers, and only in the fourth place, I guess, does one need money or a defense budget to buy planes and tanks and guns, and what have you. This is my order of priorities.

You will not win a war against somebody or deter the Soviet Union from doing something, something evil, just by presenting them with a calculation of how many dollars or deutschmarks we have spent for our defenses. We will deter them by showing them that we actually can defend ourselves, and this is being done by men and not by invoices.

At the risk of the Soviets' clapping their hands right now, I will add a rather disappointing remark, because obviously the consequence of what I have just said leads to the reintroduction of the draft in the United States. I think it's a matter for you to decide, not for us, but I can assure you that it would impress the Soviets deeply if you did. It would impress your European allies. You need not make so many speeches and gestures; just do this and it would possibly have moral advantages as well. This, now, I say as a European, and I know that the English and the Americans have different traditions in that field: But I am not so sure about the morality of letting regular soldiers defend one's country and just comforting oneself by telling oneself that one has paid so and so many dollars for defense to the internal revenue.

Now a last word about leadership. Of course, in all these fields leadership is needed. Men like George Marshall or Ernest Bevin, Jean Monnet, Charles DeGaulle — frequently it has come from the United States, from Kennedy, from Nixon, from Ford, from Kissinger, just to mention a few people — were leaders in the real sense of the word. On the other hand, I know that many Americans find it a burden to have to carry responsibility for the whole world, and certainly it is a burden. And from time to time, some Americans are tempted to pursue isolationist ideas, and from time to time other Americans are tempted to play the big boss. Both these attitudes don't have much to do with leadership. Many Europeans, I must confess, find it disagreeable to accommodate to American leadership. On the other hand, they feel that leadership among free and sovereign nations cannot consist of instructions and orders, press releases, television interviews, either in the political or in the military or in the economic field; it must be based on discussion, on questions and answers, new questions, new answers. Finally, consensus must be based on the principle of give and take.

It's your economic strength as well as your military and political power which at this present moment of history does predestine the United States to lead. This is how we in Europe see it, although we don't like to admit it. We even may say publicly that we don't like it, but we understand it as a necessity. This is how the Japanese see it, although they don't like it either — even if they don't say so publicly.

On the other hand, the vitality of your nation, your very young nation, makes it easier for you to take the lead, and beyond that you have to know that if America fails in leadership of the group of industrialized democracies — which is not just the member states of the North Atlantic Alliance, but would also have to comprise Japan — there will be nobody else to take it up. So leadership is a precious thing. You mustn't throw it away; you mustn't let leadership be dissipated by loose talk or by inaction. One can lose leadership easily. But right now in this moment of history there is nobody who would be able to take it up.

But in order to execute your leadership you are not exempt from advice. Leadership has to do with discussion and consensus by discussion. And this is exactly the point where your task comes into focus. In an open and democratic society no leader can make a decision alone. No leader is exempt from criticism. A leader needs to convince and carry his own people; it's our peoples who are choosing and influencing their leaders, and so will you be doing. And the same is true in a group of fifteen sovereign nations. Please see to it that you are well prepared to analyze and judge, and then make your influence felt. A leading nation has to know and to understand the world outside its borders. Please make sure that you sincerely try to understand the world outside the American borders and never forget that leadership in a group of sovereign nations can only be exercised if it includes advice and consent, to use the phrase of your constitution.

Now, I don't know if it's necessary in the end, to prevent a misreading of my talk, ladies and gentlemen, but just in order to assure you, you have been listening to a man who never has suffered from any inferiority complex, not *vis-à-vis* you Americans, but also not *vis-à-vis* the Russian military machine nor *vis-à-vis* the ideological impact that communism could make — no complex, for a couple of reasons, one of them being that I am a citizen of a state that is allied to the United States of America, allied to other friends in Western Europe, the French in particular, a state that is a member of a great alliance that has served all of us well for over thirty-five years — the most successful alliance of the nineteenth and twentieth centuries together in preserving peace for its members. And because I know that my own people and my own territory will be defended not only by our soldiers but also by the Alliance, at least I say this within brackets, as long as my own people provide their fair share toward that effort.

Now I hope I have given enough substance for argument, for doubt, for contradiction, for questions. I would like in the end to quote my friend Lord Carrington, who will soon become General Secretary of the North Atlantic Alliance. He said recently in an article: "We are now in a position of considerable strength. But of course, confidence should not shade into complacency. It is perhaps a good moment to reflect coolly on the strength of the West as well as on our weaknesses and compare them with those of Russia." And he talks of worrying about the situation where, he says, "solid simple facts seem to be in danger of erosion by a potent combination of passionate political advocacy and technocratic obscurity." And he says that it seems to him extraordinary and against the dictates of common sense and against the evidence of our own eyes for anyone to claim that in military terms the Western alliance is in danger of sinking to its knees. He underlines the necessity of sobriety and common resolution and says that the West would make a major mistake if it were to reduce East–West diplomacy to nothing but nuclear accountancy. And he ends by saying that the public are understandably concerned if their own nerve of nuclear competition is overexposed. We must take a broad view that dehumanization of the East–West relationship would be the quickest road to catastrophy. Sound common sense is being called for. So far Peter Carrington.

I agree with all that my friend says here. I am aware that tonight I have spoken to posterity, because all of you students will have to work for a world to come, a world the shape of which may just be emerging from the upheavals of the presently dangerous situation of our global society and our global economy. Let it be a world of peace. Let it be a world of mutual understanding, a world of freedom and humanity. In all dangers, there is always also a chance. And there is a chance if we really and sincerely try to learn lessons from history.

THE TANNER LECTURERS

1976–77

OXFORD   Bernard Williams, Cambridge University

MICHIGAN   Joel Feinberg, University of Arizona
"Voluntary Euthanasia and the Inalienable Right to Life"

STANFORD   Joel Feinberg, University of Arizona
"Voluntary Euthanasia and the Inalienable Right to Life"

1977–78

OXFORD   John Rawls, Harvard University

MICHIGAN   Sir Karl Popper, University of London
"Three Worlds"

STANFORD   Thomas Nagel, Princeton University

1978–79

OXFORD   Thomas Nagel, Princeton University
"The Limits of Objectivity"

CAMBRIDGE   C. C. O'Brien, London

MICHIGAN   Edward O. Wilson, Harvard University
"Comparative Social Theory"

STANFORD   Amartya Sen, Oxford University
"Equality of What?"

UTAH   Lord Ashby, Cambridge University
"The Search for an Environmental Ethic"

UTAH STATE   R. M. Hare, Oxford University
"Moral Conflicts"

1979–80

OXFORD   Jonathan Bennett, Univ. of British Columbia
"Morality and Consequences"

CAMBRIDGE   Raymond Aron, Collège de France
"Arms Control and Peace Research"

HARVARD   George Stigler, University of Chicago
"Economics or Ethics?"

MICHIGAN   Robert Coles, Harvard University
                "Children as Moral Observers"

STANFORD   Michel Foucault, Collège de France
                *"Omnes et Singulatim: Towards a Criticism
                of 'Political Reason'"*

UTAH   Wallace Stegner, Los Altos Hills, California
                *"The Twilight of Self-Reliance: Frontier Values
                and Contemporary America"*

1980–81

OXFORD   Saul Bellow, University of Chicago
                "A Writer from Chicago"

CAMBRIDGE   John A. Passmore, Australian National University
                "The Representative Arts as a Source of Truth"

HARVARD   Brian M. Barry, University of Chicago
                *"Do Countries Have Moral Obligations? The Case
                of World Poverty"*

MICHIGAN   John Rawls, Harvard University
                "The Basic Liberties and Their Priority"

STANFORD   Charles Fried, Harvard University
                "Is Liberty Possible?"

UTAH   Joan Robinson, Cambridge University
                "The Arms Race"

HEBREW UNIV.   Solomon H. Snyder, Johns Hopkins University
                "Drugs and the Brain and Society"

1981–82

OXFORD   Freeman Dyson, Princeton University
                "Bombs and Poetry"

CAMBRIDGE   Kingman Brewster, President Emeritus, Yale University
                "The Voluntary Society"

HARVARD   Murray Gell-Mann, California Institute of Technology
                "The Head and the Heart in Policy Studies"

MICHIGAN   Thomas C. Schelling, Harvard University
                "Ethics, Law, and the Exercise of Self-Command"

STANFORD   Alan A. Stone, Harvard University
                "Psychiatry and Morality"

UTAH R. C. Lewontin, Harvard University
"Biological Determinism"

AUSTRALIAN
NATL. UNIV. Leszek Kolakowski, Oxford University
"The Death of Utopia Reconsidered"

1982–83

OXFORD Kenneth J. Arrow, Stanford University
"The Welfare-Relevant Boundaries of the Individual"

CAMBRIDGE H. C. Robbins Landon, University College, Cardiff
*"Haydn and Eighteenth-Century Patronage
in Austria and Hungary"*

HARVARD Bernard Williams, Cambridge University
"Morality and Social Justice"

STANFORD David Gauthier, University of Pittsburgh
"The Incompleat Egoist"

UTAH Carlos Fuentes, Princeton University
"A Writer from Mexico"

JAWAHARLAL
NEHRU UNIV. Ilya Prigogine, University of Brussels
"Only an Illusion"

1983–84

OXFORD Donald D. Brown, Carnegie Institution of Washington,
Baltimore

CAMBRIDGE Stephen J. Gould, Harvard University
"Evolutionary Hopes and Realities"

HARVARD Kenneth J. Arrow, Stanford University

MICHIGAN Herbert A. Simon, Carnegie-Mellon University
*"Scientific Literacy as a Goal in a High-Technology
Society"*

STANFORD Leonard B. Meyer, University of Pennsylvania
"Ideology and Music in the Nineteenth Century"

UTAH Helmut Schmidt, former Chancellor, West Germany
"The Future of the Atlantic Alliance"

HELSINKI Georg Henrik von Wright, Helsinki
"Of Human Freedom"

1984–85

OXFORD   Barrington Moore, Harvard University

CAMBRIDGE   Amartya K. Sen, Oxford University
              "The Standard of Living"

HARVARD   Quentin Skinner, Cambridge University
              "The Paradoxes of Political Liberty"

              Kenneth J. Arrow, Stanford University

MICHIGAN   Nadine Gordimer, South Africa
              "The Essential Gesture: Writers and Responsibility"

STANFORD   Michael Slote, University of Maryland

UTAH   Laurence H. Tribe, Harvard University

1985–86

OXFORD   Thomas M. Scanlon, Harvard University

CAMBRIDGE   Aldo Van Eyck, The Netherlands

HARVARD   Michael Walter, Princeton University

MICHIGAN   Clifford Geertz, Princeton University

INDEX TO VOLUME VI, 1985

THE TANNER LECTURES ON HUMAN VALUES

A

Abelson, Robert, on scripts and plans, 39

Ability, and problem of freedom, 112

Abortion, 88; abuses of, 89

Acceptability, principle of, 190–92

Achebe, Chinua, 8

Actions, 113–14, 116; causal prerequisite for, 148; as contingent, 121–22, 125–26; as events in space and time, 111; fortuitous, 126–27, 152, 162–63; generic, 113–14, 118, 125, 136; individual, 113, 115; as over-determined, 134; vs. reactions, 125; reflex, 147, 163; as self-determined, 123, 125–26; somatic aspect of, 148–49, 162–65, 168, 170. *See also* somatic state

Activism, writing as form of, 8–11

Adaptation, 58–59, 61–62, 66–67

Adequacy of defense, principle of, 189

Aging process, 92

Akhmatova, Anna, 18

Allometry, 62

Altruism, 70

Alvarez, Luis W., 64

Animal behavior, *vis-à-vis* human, 169–70

Apartheid, 9, 14–15; as writers' material, 18

Apollonian classicism, 23

Apotheosis, 45

Appoggiaturas, 44; defined, 33, 35; examples of, 36; prevalence of, in Romanticism, 36–37

Aristotle, on necessity, 124

Arms limitation, 180; and goal of balance, 180; neglect of, 178

Art, as freedom of spirit, 9

Art of Fugue (Bach), thematic transformation in, 51

Artificial insemination, 86, 88

Atlantic Alliance, 174, 186; domination as source of corruption in, 187–88; economic deficiencies in, 178–80; evolution of grand strategy of, 173–76; leadership in, 193–94; strategic crises endured by, 176–77; strengths of, 195–96

Atonality, 51–52

B

Bach, Johann Sebastian, 51

Balance of power, 190

Barthes, Roland, on writers, 3–4

Baruch Plan, 173

Bayley, John, on Anna Akhmatova, 18

Beckett, Samuel, 16–17

Beethoven, Ludwig von, 50–51

Beginnings of life, moral issues concerning, 89

Belinsky, Vissarion, on poets, 14

Bellow, Saul, 4

Benjamin, Walter, 19

Berger, John, 4

Bevin, Ernest, 193

Bioethics, 89–91, 93

Biological units, 68–70

Biological warfare, 91

Biotechnology. *See* genetic engineering

Bloom, Allan, on man, 24

Böll, Heinrich, 14

Borges, Jorge Luis, 6

Botany, 96

Boveri, Theodore, 97
Brahms, Johannes, use of axial melodies by, 42
Brain, nature of, 67–68
Brandt, Willy, 185–86
Breytenbach, Breyten, 13
Brezhnev, Leonid, 176
Brutus, Dennis, 13

C

Callaghan, James, 185
Camus, Albert, 6–7, 10
Cancer, 92, 98
Cardenal, Ernesto, 8
Carrington, Lord Peter, on Atlantic Alliance, 195–96
Carter, Jimmy (President), 176
Causal history, 167
Causal mechanism, 161
Causes: as action stimulant, 148; anterior, 166; chain of, 161
Céline, Louis Ferdinand, 16
Cell, metabolization of drugs in, 98
Chekhov, Anton, 18–19
Chomskian linguistics, 51
Chromosome diminution, 96–97
Classical music, 32; syntactic closure in, 42, 44; syntactic scripts in, 40, 45–46
Classicism, elements of, 23
Cloning, 82, 84, 88
Coleridge, Samuel Taylor, on organicism, 29
Comecon, 181
Commands, 156; as reasons, 156
Communism, 183
Compatibility thesis, 151–52
Complementarity, 78; base, 82
Compulsion, 117–18, 170
Conflict, as writer's matrix, 7, 14–15, 19
Congenital abnormalities, 94. *See also* genetic abnormalities
Congruence, 162; in causality, 152–53
Consciousness: evolution of, 64, 66; human, 63, 68–71; and religion, 68

Consensus, 144–46
Constraints, syntactic, 39; of tonality. *See* tonality
Containment, policy of, 174
Context, of actions, 153–54; as determined by ends, 155; explanations as, 164; as self-contained, 154
Contingency, 123; as a condition, 126. *See also* actions, as contingent
Continuous reevaluation, principle of, 189
Contraception, 93
Conventional weapons, 188
Creativity: integrity in, 12; as primal spout, 17; pure form of, 3, 8, 17; tension as matrix of, 3, 19
Credibility, principle of, 189, 191
Cretaceous extinctions, 59, 64–65
Crick, Francis, 78
Cronin, Jeremy, 13
Cuban missile crisis, 174, 176
Cystic fibrosis, 80, 92
Czerny, Carl, on Beethoven, 50

D

DNA, 101–2, 104; base, 78; double-helical structure of, 77–78; encoding of protein by, 78–80, 104; functions of, 77–78; nucleotides, 78; recombinant, 82–83, 104
Dadaists, 15–16
Darwin, Charles, 55, 57; on the origin of species, 62–63
Darwinism, 55–58, 62–63; relationship of, to laissez-faire economics, 57
Dawid, Igor, 97
Dawkins, Richard, 60
DeGaulle, Charles, 185
Debussy, Claude, 37; use of motivic constancy by, 38
Deficit spending, 178; effect on world of U.S., 179; Keynesian, 178
Descartes, René, 110, 150; on freedom, 170
D'Estaing, Giscard, 185
Détente: German view of, 186; as official NATO strategy, 176; Soviet errors in, 181; Western errors in, 180

Determinism, 150, 162; in causal history, 167; vs. fatalism, 152; vs. freedom of the will, 111; as heuristic maxim, 168; mechanistic, 150–51; prestige of, 152; as world view, 110

Deterrence, 191, 193; nuclear, 188; principle of, 189

Dhlomo, H. I. E., 10

Diabetes, 80, 92

Die Meistersinger (Wagner), melodic stretching in, 37

Die Walküre (Wagner), gap-fill melodies in, 38; statistical form in, 47–48

Dionysian Romanticism, 23

Disestablishment, 16

Dulles, John Foster, 174; roll back strategy of, 174

Dynamic curve, defined, 47

E

East–West relationship, 186, 196

Economy, world. *See* Atlantic Alliance, economic deficiencies in

Embryogenesis, 94–95

Embryology, history of, 94–95

Ends, 154; as ultimate values, 130–31

Enzymes, 80

Equilibrium, principle of, 190

Europe, 184; consistent foreign policy of, 185–86; as economically sick, 186; historical experience of, 184–5, 187; and the Soviet Union, 185; and the United States, 194

European Community, 186

Evolution, concept of, 55; of mammals with dinosaurs, 65

Evolutionary theory, 55–59

Exchange rates, 179

Exaptation, 66–67

Expectations: as reasons, 143; reasons based on, 132–33

Explanations: of actions, 134; causal, 163, 165; as establishing facts, 136–37, 139; as excuses, 135; periodicity of, 59; as predictive, 140; reason-, 163–65; types of, 136

Extinction, 69; of dinosaurs, 65

F

Final Act of Helsinki, 176

Fischer, Ernst, on artistic freedom, 8–9

Fitness, Darwinian, 70

Flaubert, Gustav, on the impersonality of art, 15

Flexible response, strategy of, 175, 188

Flute Quartet in A (Mozart), gap-fill melodies in, 44

Ford, Gerald (President), 177, 193

Form, in musical composition, 25

Four-Power Agreement, 176

Fourth Symphony (Brahms), axial melodies in, 42

Fourth Symphony (Mahler), 45; gap-fill melodies and melodic stretching in, 44; statistical form in, 47

Free will. *See* freedom of the will

Freedom, 112; of action, 121, 128; actual vs. potential, 116–17; attempt to define, 119–20; of choice, 121, 128; vs. determinism, 151–52, 163, 165–66; education as enhancing, 116; as illusion, 151, 168; restrictions on, 117–18, 124, 127

Freedom of the will, 110, 149–50, 168; as classical problem, 109–11; vs. determinism, 111

Freud, Sigmund, on individuality, 26

Freudian psychology, 51

G

Gall, Joseph, 97

Gene alteration, 97

Gene amplification, 97–98

Gene clustering, 103–4

Gene encoding, 97

Gene expression, 78–79, 94, 96, 99, 101, 103–4

Gene isolation, 82

Gene splicing, 102

Gene therapy, 89–90

Genetic abnormalities, 88–90

Genetic biochemistry, 96, 104

Genetic drift, 58–59, 61

Genetic engineering, 77, 79, 81; in agriculture, 85, 86, 93; with animals, 86;

benefits of, 90–93; dangers of, 83–85, 90–91, 93; and oil spills, 85; applications of, to warfare, 92
Genetic rearrangement, 99–100
Genetic reproduction, 77, 79
Genetic transposability, 99–100
Genetic variation, 56–58
Genetics, future of, 105–6
German treaties, 176
German–Polish Agreement, 176
Germany: acceptability principle as important to, 192; misunderstanding of position of, 186–87; need for draft in, 192–93; peace movement in, 192
Glass, Philip, as minimalist composer, 52
Grass, Günter, 14

H

Harmel Report, 176
Harmel, Pierre, 176
Heart disease, 80
Hemophilia, 77, 80
Hormones, 105
Hugo, Victor, on conventionality, 25
Huxley, Julian, 56, 62; on modern synthesis, 55

I

Iconoclasts, 15–16
Immunology, 96
Imperialism, 182
Inability, and problem of freedom, 112
Incompatibility thesis, 151
Indeterminism, 167; in physics, 151
Inhibition, defined, 118
Innervations, as causal, 153–55, 158, 161–62, 164
Insulin, 80–82
Integrity, and the writer in society, 7
Interest rates, increase in, 178
Interferon, 82–83
International commerce, deterioration of, 179

J

Joyce, James, 5–6, 16–17

K

Kafka, Franz, 16
Kant, Immanuel, on noumenal world, 111
Keane, Molly, 4
Kennan, George, on containment, 174
Kennedy, John F. (President), 174, 186, 194
Kerouac, Jack, 16
Keynes, J. M., 178
Kissinger, Henry, 173, 177, 187, 193; on dominance, 187; on the deficit, 179
Koestler, Arthur, 57
Kohl, Helmut, 186
Kundera, Milan, 6, 9–10

L

La Guma, Alex, 13
Language, as writer's corpus, 4, 14
Laplace, Pierre Simon de, on determinism, 167
Law of Causation, 111–12
Laws of nature, 167–68, 170
Leadership: American, 194; by consensus, 194–95
Leitmotives, defined, 37
Leninism, 183
Les Preludes (Liszt), axial melodies in, 41–42
Lichtenthal, Peter: on the sublime, 48; on unity, 51
"Liebestod" (Wagner), statistical form in, 47–49
Lies, 146; as obscuring reasons, 139–40, 143, 168
Liszt, Franz, 48; on Chopin, 25; on originality, 25; use of axial melodies by, 42
Literary style, as transformer of world, 15–16

Lovejoy, Arthur O., on self-realization, 29–30

Loyalty, as an emotion, 7

M

Macroevolution, 57–58

Madingoane, Ngoapele, 8

Mahler, Gustav, 44, 47

Manipulation, defined, 165–66

Marriage of Figaro (Mozart), changing-note schema in, 40

Marshall Plan, 173–74

Marshall, George, 193

Marxism, 183

Mattera, Don, 10

Mayr, Ernst, on modern synthesis, 55–56

McClintock, Barbara, 98–99

McNamara, Robert S., initiation of flexible response by, 175

Mechanistic world-view, 110

Melodic stretching, 33, 37; defined, 32; and Romanticism, 32, 34–35, 37

Melody, 35; axial, 40–43; changing-note, 40, 42–43; gap-fill, 36, 37, 39, 43–44; as Romantic ideal of musical expression, 31–32; stretching in. *See* melodic stretching

Mendelian genetics, 77, 80

Mental acts, 149

Metaphor, as conceptual mythology, 143

Military deterrence, strategy of, 175

Military strategy: need for new, 188; principles of, 189–90

Milosz, Czeslaw, 6

Mitterrand, François, 185

Modern synthesis, 55, 57–58; criticisms of, 58–63

Mofolo, Thomas, 10

Molecular embryology, 105

Monnet, Jean, 193

Moore, G. E., 151; on freedom, 121; on the material world, 110

Morrison, Toni, 4

Motivation: as background, 155, 157, 161; as complex, 132, 134, 144; substrate of, 157–58, 159, 161

Motives, 131–32, 140

Mozart, Wolfgang Amadeus: use of changing-note schema by, 40; use of melodic stretching by, 32–33

Musical cessation, 47; as distinguished from closure, 47–49

Mutation, 82, 95, 99–100, 105–6

N

NATO (North Atlantic Treaty Organization), 176

Natural selection, 55–59, 61–62, 64, 67

Neo-Darwinism, 56

Neontony, 67

Nervous system, 148–50, 155; programming of, 156–57, 159, 162, 166

Neural states, as criteria of reasons, 160

Nixon, Richard M. (President), 176–77, 194

Non-proliferation treaty, 176

Norm-authorities, 118, 120

Norms, 119–20; as deontic, 117; internalized, 119; as prohibitions, 117; as societal, 119; as sources of action, 119–20

North-Atlantic Pact, 180

Nouveau roman writers, 15

Nuclear competition, 196

Nuclear freeze, American proposals for, 191

Nuclear retaliation, strategy of, 174–75

Nuclear weapons, European reliance on, 188

O

Obligations, 117–18

Octet in F Major (Schubert), changing-note schema in, 40

Omission, 118; ability in, 127; vs. action, 114; inability in, 115–16; as mode of action, 120, 122–23, 126; vs. performance, 149; vs. prohibitions, 117

Organic model, vs. language model, 28–29

Organicism, 31–32; core metaphor of, 29; as goal-directed, 29; persistence of, 28; as Platonism, 50; as serialism, 51. *See also* Romanticism, organicism as part of

Otello (Verdi), melodic stretching in, 35–36; statistical form in, 47

Overspecialization, 69

P

Parallelism, 152–53, 157

Paz, Octavio, on function of writers, 14

Penicillin, 80

Philosophy, 109; change in, 110; as demystification, 143; scientific, 150; theological, 150

Physics, role of, in indeterminism, 151

Plaatje, Solomon T., 10

Plan, as applied to composition, 41; defined, 39–40

Plantinga, Leon, 25

Politburo, 181, 183

Polymers, 78

Polyproteins, 103

Pompidou, Georges, 185

Pound, Ezra, 9

Preadaptation, 66–67

Prevention, as concept, 115, 117–18

Primary parameters, 46

Prohibitions, 117–18

Promises, 140; expectation as basis for, 143; as reasons, 133, 139–40

Protectionism, 179

Public opinion, and military strategy, 191

Punctuated equilibrium, 60

R

RNA, 97, 101–4, 106

Rationality, 128–29; as ideal, 130

Ratner, Leonard, 47; on musical structure, 28

Reaction, 125

Reagan, Ronald (President), 178

Reason, defined, 128

Reasons, 130–31, 135; and actions, 123–24, 128–30, 133–34, 142–44, 147; vs. cause, 124, 129; chain of, 161; choosing among, 127; as compelling, 124, 133–34; criteria for existence of, 159–61; efficacious, 135, 137, 156; as evolving from norms, 120, 127–28; vs. motives, 131–32

Reich, Steve, as minimalist composer, 52

Religious leaders, and military strategy, 191

Responsibility: as imposed by society, 4, 6–8, 10–11, 13; as orthodoxy, 11–12; as part of creative act, 3

Restrictions, 117

Ribosomes, 97–98, 103

Rieff, Philip, 26

Romantic music, 32; general plans in, 40, 46; weakness of closure in, 42, 44–45

Romantic poetry, 30–31

Romanticism, 24; axial melodies as consistent with, 42; elements of, 23–26, 30–32, 37, 48; ideology of, 51; organicism as part of, 27–28; originality as ideology of, 26–27; persistence of, 52; unity in, 50

Rousseau, Jean Jacques, on politics, 24

Russia: historical imperialism of, 182, 185; Western need to contain, 184; world-wide cultural influence of, 183

Russians: motivation of, 183

S

SALT negotiations, 176–77, 180

Sacrifice, as moral authority, 13

Sand, George, 15

Schank, Roger, on scripts and plans, 39

Schenkerian music, 51

Schizophrenia, 92

Schlegel, August Wilhelm, on form, 27–28

Schopenhauer, Arthur, on melody, 31–32

Schubert, Franz: use of axial melodies by, 40–41; use of changing-note scheme by, 40

Schumann, Robert, 47; on Chopin, 30; on Romantic music, 25–26; use of melodic stretching by, 33–35

Science: compartmentalization of, 95–96; regulation of, 93

Script, as applied to composition, 41; defined, 39–40; syntactic, 43–44

Secondary parameters: absence of closure in, 49; as statistical, 46; as values of Romanticism, 47, 50

Self-determination, 116, 128, 152; as reasoned, 124–26

Self-expression, 30

Self-image, 141

Self-realization, 30

Self-understanding, 138, 140, 143, 169; subconscious, 142

Serote, Mongane, 13

Selfish genes, concept of, 60–61, 69

Shifting balance theory, 61

Sickle cell anemia, 77, 80, 100

Silk, genetic structure of, 102–3

Smith, Adam, 57–58

Social criticism, grammar and meanings in, 14

Social realism, demands of, 13–14

Sociobiology, 70

Somatic state, 166, 168; as causally unique, 167

Sontag, Susan, 4; on the cultural revolution, 16

Soviet Union, 175, 193; historical imperialism of, 181; military expansion by, 180–81 (*See also* Russia); relationship of Atlantic Alliance with, 180; observance of treaties by, 181

Soyinka, Wole, 8

Speciation, 59

Stalin, Joseph, 174, 183; U.S. perception of, 182

Statistical climax, 45, 47–48

Statistical form, 49–50; vs. syntactic form, 48

Steiner, George, on writing, 13–14

Stoutland, Frederick, on problem of congruence, 112

String Quintet in C Major (Schubert), axial melodies in, 40–41

String Quintet in G Minor (Mozart), melodic stretching in, 32–33

Subsidence, 45, 47

Subsidization, 179

Supply-side economics, 178

Surrogate motherhood, 86, 88

Symbolists, 15–16

Syntactic climax, defined, 46

Syntactic form, 46; vs. statistical form, 48

Syntax, 33, 45; as source of constraint, 46; as source of convention, 35–37, 46; in musical composition, 25

Synthesis, of creativity and social responsibility, 8

T

Taylor, Maxwell D., on nuclear war, 174–75

Test ban treaty, 176

Thatcher, Margaret, 179, 185

Thematic transformation, as unifying, 50

Thibaut, Anton, on music, 24

Third Piano Concerto (Beethoven), as example of unity, 50–51

Tonality, 25, 27

Tournier, Michel, on writer's responsibility, 17

Transcriptional control, 101

Translational amplification, 103

"Träumerei" (Schumann), melodic stretching in, 33–34; statistical form in, 47

Truth: as absolute, 146; vs. consensus, 144–45; as correctness of understanding, 141–42, 144; as metaphor, 142; as obscure, 143; as public knowledge, 141; self-deception as obscuring, 142; self-knowledge in, 140–41

U

Understanding, 156; as achieved by efficaciousness, 137; as consensus, 138; conversion as means of, 140–

44; levels of, 137–38; as metaphor, 156; as needing subject, 138

United Nations Charter, 181

United States: in the Atlantic Alliance, 173; cooperation of, with Soviet Union, 175, 180; effect of economic behavior of, 179; inconsistent foreign policy of, 186; misunderstanding of Europe by, 185, 187; need for draft in, 193; optimism of, 184; unilateral action by, 175, 178; as world leader, 194

Unity, musical, 50–51

Updike, John, 5

V

Van Schlegel, Friederich, on Romantic poetry, 30–31

Verdi, Giuseppe, 47; use of melodic stretching by, 35–36

Vietnam War, 177

Vonnegut, Kurt, Jr., 4

W

Wagner, Richard, 37, 47; on art, 25; on composition, 29; use of gap-fill melodies by, 37–38

Watergate, 177

Watson, James, 78

Webern, Anton, 51; on Bach, 51

Wilson, Harold, 185

Woolf, Virginia, 15

Wright, Sewall, 61

Writers: exile as shaping, 5–6; role of, in social conflict, 5, 7; as social beings, 4, 19; as transforming the world, 17

Writing, as essential gesture, 4–5, 10–12

X

Xenakis, Iannis, as statistical composer, 52

THE TANNER LECTURES ON HUMAN VALUES, Volume VI,
was composed in Intertype Garamond with Garamond Foundry display type
by Donald M. Henriksen, Scholarly Typography, Salt Lake City.

DISCARD